Embracing
Our Inheritance

[Handwritten inscription:]

Fr. Kim,

Thank you for being an example of how God has called us.

Continue our Story of Faith

[Signature]

Embracing
Our Inheritance

Jubilee Reflections on
Korean American Catholics
(1966–2016)

Edited by
Simon C. Kim
and
Francis Daeshin Kim

Foreword by
William T. Cavanaugh

ᏜPICKWICK *Publications* · Eugene, Oregon

Pickwick Publications
An Imprint of Wipf and Stock Publishers
199 W. 8th Ave., Suite 3
Eugene, OR 97401

www.wipfandstock.com

PAPERBACK ISBN: 978-1-4982-8286-4
HARDCOVER ISBN: 978-1-4982-8288-8
EBOOK ISBN: 978-1-4982-8287-1

Cataloguing-in-Publication data:

Names: Kim, Simon C. | Kim, Francis Daeshin | Cavanaugh, William T.

Title: Embracing Our Inheritance : Jubilee Reflections on Korean American Catholics (1966–2016) / edited by Simon C. Kim and Francis Daeshin Kim ; foreword by William T. Cavanaugh.

Description: Eugene, OR: Pickwick Publications, 2016 | Includes bibliographical references.

Identifiers: ISBN 978-1-4982-8286-4 (paperback) | ISBN 978-1-4982-8288-8 (hardcover) | ISBN 978-1-4982-8287-1 (ebook)

Subjects: LCSH: Catholic Church Korea—History—20th century.

CLASSIFICATION: BX1670.5 .E52 2016 (PRINT)

Manufactured in the U.S.A.   JUNE 17, 2016

Dedicated to Korean American Catholics
past, present, and future

Contents

Foreword

IT HAS BEEN MY privilege to listen in on the conversation among
Korean American Catholic scholars that has led to this book. I
have one foot out of and one foot in this conversation—my ancestors are from Ireland, Germany, and Poland, but I share the same
Catholic faith as the authors collected here. I have learned much
about the Korean American experience from these scholars, but
I have learned about the Catholic experience more generally as
well. Catholicism names the attempt to hear distinctly the part that
every people and every person is playing in God's symphony. The
simultaneous unity and diversity of that symphony makes the part
played by Korean American Catholics of interest not just to that
community but to anyone interested in the Catholic experience.

The goal of the Center for World Catholicism and Intercultural Theology at DePaul University—of which I am Director and
which sponsored the conference from which this book arose—is
to promote the study of Catholicism in non-European and non-
North American contexts, the "global South" as it is called, for lack
of a better term. As we recognize, however, the South is already in
the North, and the kinds of encounter that this produces allows for
a new appreciation of the mixedness—or *mestizaje*, as Latino theologians say—that is at the heart of the Catholic way of viewing and
experiencing the world. Though *mestizos* were often deprecated as
impure, mixedness is in fact privileged in Catholic tradition: Abraham was an immigrant, Jesus is both divine and human, and every
instantiation of Catholicism in every part of the world is both part

of a universal tradition and an inculturation of that tradition in the ways of life of a particular people. As the essays in this book attest, the Korean American Catholic experience is an attempt to live out that unity in diversity that has characterized Catholicism since its beginning.

The chapters of this volume reflect on the Korean American Catholic experience through stories of that experience, in personal narratives, historical accounts, and sociological data. Stories shape identity, and it is important that Korean American Catholics claim their identity to resist a bland assimilation and secularization into American society. At the same time, however, the essays here collected show that identity is not a fixed thing; identity is sometimes found not in staying put but in going forth. If contemporary South Korea is both deeply traditional (one must learn with how many hands to hold one's cup if an elder is pouring, as I learned on a visit to Seoul) and rapidly changing (South Korea has been named the "Most Wired" country in the world), Koreans in America and their descendants also grapple with adapting tradition to a new context. As the critical yet confident essays in this volume make clear, however, the movement of Korean American Catholics is a movement of the Holy Spirit, not so much to be resisted as to be embraced as an opportunity for service to God and to others, both within and without the Korean American Catholic community.

In the end, then, this is a book of theology, a book not just about a community of people but about God, specifically the universal God who became incarnated in a particular human being— Jesus Christ—and cast the Spirit across the whole created world. The authors in this volume deftly take up traditional theological themes and traditional texts—Scripture, Augustine, Aquinas, etc.—to weave the story of Korean American Catholics into the wider story of what God is doing in human history. The result is a book that will be of interest to both scholars and to people in the pews, who can read vitality and hope in its pages.

William T. Cavanaugh, DePaul University
Center for World Catholicism and Intercultural Theology

Preface

A GLARING OMISSION THAT readers may immediately notice about this collected work is the absence of a female contributor. This was not intentional. The original plan was to include female perspectives, but none have ended up in the final product. First, this lack reminds us that the female voice must be better encouraged, and perhaps better nurtured in future generations, especially in immigrant cultural groups. At the onset of this project, a female contributor was present; however, she was only able to journey with us approximately two–thirds of the way before having to tend to personal matters. Even without this important voice, our group was blessed with scholars representing the spectrum of generations (1.5, 2nd and even 3rd). Therefore, I cannot express enough gratitude to the scholars God has surrounded us with, not only in this project but for many future endeavors as well.

The Korean American Catholic Jubilee is not a celebration for just a single immigrant religious group in the United States. Rather, this commemoration of fifty years in the United States is also a reminder that other ethnic faith groups have a similar occasion to celebrate, since the US social and ecclesial landscape shifted so dramatically in the mid–1960s. Preparations for this historical milestone involved a collaborative effort from both the laity and clergy. In particular, the Korean American Catholic Forum involving both lay and priest theologians met regularly the past couple of years in anticipation of the jubilee. The task given to this group was to theologically reflect on the presence of Korean American

Catholics as an ethnic faith group emerging as their own distinct people after half a century.

In 2013, the Korean American Priests Association (KAPA) made conscious decisions on behalf of the presbyterate and the communities they represented. The first decision was to use the historical marker set by the Archdiocese of San Francisco in 1966. Although other faith communities of Korean descent existed prior to this year, they were not officially acknowledged in the US church until an Archbishop from the Bay area officially recognized Korean Catholic immigrants in his archdiocese. Thus, KAPA's decision to honor 50 years of ministry in the Korean American Catholic communities in 2016 helped make this a national celebration for both the local communities as well as the church at large.

The second crucial decision by KAPA was at the November board meeting of that same year when priests representing their regional districts unanimously agreed to call themselves Korean American Catholics rather than common expressions highlighting their immigrant status or their presence as simply extensions of the people in Korea (*kyopo*). Even priests working in the United States but belonging to dioceses overseas agreed upon this new name highlighting the differences of the people they were ministering to because of the immigration experience. Thus, KAPA's decision to use "Korean American Catholics" signified the emergence of a cultural faith group similar to those back in the homeland, but at the same time, different because of the heritage of their host country.

As a response to these two decisions, Fr. Alex K. Kim (KAPA President, 2014) and Fr. Eun Keun Shin (KAPA Chairman, 2014) supported my idea of bringing scholars together to theologically reflect on the Korean American Catholic experience. I am truly grateful to these two men and the entire organization for their priestly support in our campaign. In March 2014, theologians gathered at the Mexican American Catholic College in San Antonio to discern the coming together of this scholarly group. Fr. Virgilio Elizondo facilitated the first gathering, explaining the social and ecclesial processes that Hispanics/Latinos went through in the seventies. Through this initial gathering, theologians embraced the task of identifying Korean American Catholics as a culturally distinct group within a religious tradition. Therefore, we are truly grateful for the mentoring we received from such a founding member of the Hispanic/Latino community.

The second gathering was in March 2015 hosted by St. Thomas Korean Catholic Center, Anaheim and Fr. Alex Kim. This event allowed theologians to present their initial projects to see if the themes resonated with the Korean American Catholic communities, as parish council members, seminarians, religious, DREs, youth and young adults, etc., discussed and gave valuable feedback on each presentation. Without the support of local communities in Southern California, and in particular, St. Thomas and the FIAT Foundation, such an invaluable process would not have been imaginable. As a follow up in April 2015, a working group was held in Chicago to discuss the evaluations from the March gathering and to prepare for the final presentations of individual scholarly works. We were blessed with Fr. Robert Schreiter, CPPS facilitating this process and the St. Paul Chong Hasang community in Des Plaines for supporting this gathering.

On November 14, 2015, the Center for World Catholicism and Intercultural Theology (CWCIT) at DePaul University hosted the conference on the *Jubilee Reflections on Korean American Catholics*. The final papers presented that day make up the eventual chapters within this collected work. Without the support of Dr. William T. Cavanaugh and his wonderful staff, such a finale to our project would not have been possible. There are so many more people to acknowledge since several communities supported us on this journey. Both the conference and this book are wonderful fruits of our labor and important aspects in creating an institutional memory for the 2016 Jubilee celebration as well as the commemorations of future generations.

Simon C. Kim

Introduction

If you're holding this in your hands, if you're reading these words, wondering whether to buy or read this book, you're standing at a threshold. You have cracked open the door a little, and you have the opportunity to cross from not knowing, into a land of knowledge. You may even find yourself crossing from a place where you have no identity, or not even knowing that you lacked, or wanted, or *needed* an identity, to a place where you discover a people who are *celebrating* their identity. A people who not so long ago had no identity either, but who are now staking a claim, and who are building for the future. You may even find that you belong to these people. In which case you may even discover a new way of seeing the world, a new way of being in the world.

Father Simon Kim compares the plight of Korean American immigrants to that of the Israelites, who left behind their familiar environment and became strangers wandering in foreign lands. They too had to forge their own identity, their older generation too had to deal with the disconnect felt by subsequent generations born far away from the place they left behind. Korean Americans embrace certain mythical narratives about their heritage, just as the Israelites relied on their divine history. But it is the responsibility of the younger generations to preserve both their pioneering spirit and their rich culture if they are to continue in their celebrations.

It is fitting that this book begins with a chapter written by Fr. Simon, for it is he who was the most instrumental, most active, and most vocal in assembling this impressive group of priests,

Introduction

theologians, and scholars, and seeing this project through. It was always his hope that we would lay down a marker, create something of note that would celebrate fifty years of the existence of a group that calls themselves Korean American Catholic. Of course there were Korean American Catholics before 1966, but until the Archdiocese of San Francisco recognized the Korean American community as an actual entity, you could say that they didn't have an actual identity, and subsequently they became an official part of the religious landscape in the United States. The jubilee anniversary of this event is what this book serves to celebrate.

It is also fitting therefore that our next contributor is the first Korean American diocesan priest ordained in the United States. Father Paul Lee is truly a pioneer, a man brimming with a multitude of cultures and an abundance of ideas. His short paper represents only a small fraction of what he has to give (and continues to give) to our community, but it is important nonetheless. His paper shows us what a work of scholarship can do, how the theology of the Pentecost, the gift of the Spirit and the birth of the church, can be applied to the present reality of a group such as Korean American Catholics and show them the way. With penetrating insight, Fr. Paul is able to pinpoint challenges specific to Korean American Catholics, with their hard set ways and their peculiarities, but give them hope because he knows just what greatness they are capable of. He knows that Korean Americans today parallel the self-understanding of early Christians and the new community and new humanity they formed. Fr. Paul's ideas are convincing, enlightening, and true.

Speaking of truth, Dr. Chaeyoon Lim's statistical portrait of Korean American Catholics is an extraordinary paper and just as enlightening and convincing. Never underestimate the power of numbers! In a most elegant way (and in a way that some of our readers may find wonderfully geeky, or nerdy) Dr. Lim is able to paint a rich picture of life as a Korean American Catholic, purely by interpreting statistical data. He is able to show us how the challenges faced by Korean American Catholics are different to those faced by Korean American Protestants. He is able to suggest why there is a decline in religious affiliation, and why there is a rise in those who have none ("the rise of the nones"). But maybe just as importantly, he shows us how valuable the data is, and why there is a need not only of more data, but of more people such as he, who have an interest in analyzing and drawing conclusions from all that information. Korean American Catholics have a right to be proud to have such an accomplished scholar in their midst, someone with the skill with which to show people a reflection of who they are through such pictures painted with numbers, and I'm wondering if his paper won't encourage some younger readers to consider a future in such a fascinating and valuable field!

If you are a younger reader considering a future in academia, you could do a lot worse than follow the illustrious career of Dr. James Lee. If Dr. Lim is able to shine a light on truths through statistical data, Dr. Lee is a historian with the gift of shining a light on the great opportunity given to Korean American Catholics of being the bearers of history and tradition, by applying his considerable expertise in Early Christianity. Again, this is a wonderful example of the power of scholarship. He uses the thoughts of a fourth century theologian (Augustine of Hippo) and the views and beliefs of an eighteenth century Korean martyr (Augustine Jeong) to enrich the identity of Korean American Catholics and to give hope of what they can be. Further, his personal story shows the power of the Catholic tradition, for he is a convert, inspired to embrace the Catholic faith through his learning. The fact that he is not the only convert participating in this project (they include the writers of the two final papers, and even myself!) maybe gives Korean American Catholics the right to be a little hopeful, upon learning of these personal stories.

Of all the personal stories, however, I find Dr. Andrew Kim's the most fascinating. The fact that he went through such a long period of agnosticism, followed by a conversion to Catholicism, followed by impressive work in the field of theology, only to discover that his paternal grandfather whom he never met was also something of a theological scholar, is sensational. That's what heritage does! It is an undeniable force! Anyway, it is a shame that his final paper was not able to include much of the biographical narratives that were in his earlier drafts, because the personal challenges of growing up as a third generation biracial Korean American are little known to most, but this book was always intended to be one of scholarship, and I am sure his story will surface elsewhere. What it does contribute, however, is again this example of how one's academic specialty (in this case, in the thought of St. Thomas Aquinas) has a relevance to the reality facing today's Korean American Catholic. Don't be put off by such terms as "binary-oppositionalism." Armed with a dictionary, you have the chance of witnessing how one man's learning helped solve his personal issues of biracial identity, of oppositional identity. Potential scholars take note, we need more historians like this.

And so, at the end of this roster of gifted theologians with such insight into the past, we present a paper by Dr. Hoon Choi which tackles the timely, and very present issue of gender identity. Dr. Choi urges us to pay attention to our gendered selves. He wants us to pay attention to what it is to be masculine or feminine, to why we ascribe certain qualities to different genders, and to what this means for our role in society. Not only does he deal with this hot topic, but in what the editors of this book lovingly call his "Imagine!" section, he imagines the future of our church, the kind of church that we can be. He imagines us getting over our identity crises, whether of gender or culture or race, these things that we as a group struggle with, and in a veritable *tour de force* of a passage, dares to propose a radical and hopeful message for the future of Korean American Catholics. It is inspiring.

I myself have found that others are somewhat inspired by my own journey, from being involved in the youth ministry at my own Korean American parish, to attending the Korean American Catholic Forum in March of 2015 purely as an interested bystander, to being shown by these authors that there was a greater world out there and work to be done for the Korean American community, and finally somehow to being invited to actually participate in the process of this publication. I am not a priest, or scholar, or theologian. But I was flown out to Chicago to hear their latest drafts at the conference at DePaul University. I got to meet and hang out with these extraordinary thinkers there, staying up late, discussing the future of our community. And now here I am, as their co-editor, writing this introduction in the hopes that you too will cross that threshold as I did. My journey enriched my youth ministry, and in a way, my students are who this book is for. It is for the future generations, and this introduction is here to urge them, to urge you, to open the door and cross to the other side, to get to know these papers. For the future is in your hands. Literally, figuratively, and spiritually.

Francis Daeshin Kim

1

The Emergence of Korean American Catholics

Tracing the Narratives of God's People

—— Simon C. Kim ——

HUMAN BEINGS ARE INQUISITIVE creatures desiring to know their origin both as individual and communal beings. Often, this desire to know one's origin is taken for granted since individual and communal understanding derives from our families, faith, community and a nation that naturally surrounds us. When this condition is not satisfied, we become restless, seeking a deeper meaning in our lives by examining where we have come from in order to better embrace where we are headed next. Cases where there is an absence of family, faith, community and even a nation for those who were adopted, as in the case of Korean orphans, displaced from their homes by natural disasters such as Hurricane Katrina, or forced to flee as refugees from areas of heightened violence, highlight what has been taken for granted by those such as nonadoptees who do not necessarily reflect on their plight. Nevertheless, people in these types of situations remind us why the search for identity is so crucial, and what the implications are when this enterprise is not undertaken. Their journey to better understand themselves is a powerful reminder that the fulfillment of one's destiny begins with the remembrance of the past.

> Forming a sense of identity for adoptees is complicated by gaps and contradictions in autobiographical knowledge. It is difficult to establish a sense of self when one lacks information about the beginnings of life and the foundations of family relationships. The stories that adopted people tell of their lives reveal how they see themselves and how they connect themselves to the people around them. These stories make us who we are; they are the very essence of identity . . . Stories are important. Yet it is not the events themselves that matter so much, but rather the way we make sense of them.[1]

In particular, people who have been adopted tend to reveal both the aspects of longing to understand one's origin to quench the internal struggles of their identity, as well as seeking further meaning for their lives; conditions others might take for granted based on a false sense of assurance of who they really are. Based on the work, *Being Adopted: The Lifelong Search for Self*, professional counselors, Mary Kreuger and Fred Hanna conclude, "Nonadoptees may take for granted the accurate knowledge they hold about their biological heritage and family culture. In contrast, the adoptee is often expected to accept without question the stories provided along with the truths and heritage of his or her nonrelated adopted family."[2] This does not mean the nonadopted all take their heritage for granted, since some are curious enough to engage in projects reconstructing their family tree. "Not surprisingly, there seem to be many similarities between why people seek to fill in the branches of their family tree and why adoptees dig for their biological roots."[3]

---

1. Fitzhardinge, "Adoption," 66.

2. Kreuger and Hanna, "Why Adoptees Search," 195; see also Brodzinsky et al., *Being Adopted*.

3. Darongkamas and Lorenc, "Going Back to our Roots," 1022.

Utilizing Irvin Yalom's existential approach to psychotherapy,[4] Krueger and Hanna apply four concerns that lead to the search for one's identity especially in adoptees—death, isolation, freedom, and meaninglessness.[5] Coming to grips with one's mortality because of the anxiety caused by the unknowns of the afterlife can assist in searching for a meaningful life here and now. "Death has a paradoxical quality in that the fear of it is paralyzing to the individual who avoids it, while at the same time acceptance of its inevitability can free the individual from the trivial life that results from that avoidance."[6] In addition to the reality of separation in death, isolation in this life can also be a powerful factor in propelling one to search for the meaning of one's life. "The fundamental anxiety surrounding the separation between the individual and the world propels one to attempt to traverse this phenomenon by endeavoring to establish interpersonal belonging with others."[7] Freedom is also needed because this search involves two types of guilt: guilt from a feeling of betrayal of the adopted family and from not being true to oneself if the search for the past is not undertaken.[8] Finally, the desire to put meaning to even the minute details of everyday life spurs the digging into one's past.

> Meaning grounds the individual in his or her reality. Attributing meaning to one's endeavors provides structure and direction. Of course, the meaning system needs to be of one's own choosing to be authentic and fulfilling. The development of a meaning system is joined with one's struggle to make sense of his or her experience of anxiety, existential isolation, and inherent freedom.[9]

One's origins, even when unknown by both groups, are more likely questioned by only those who have been adopted, than those who were not. Thus, the adoptee's longing for identity through the

4. Yalom, *Existential Psychotherapy*.
5. Kreuger and Hanna, "Why Adoptees Search," 198.
6. Ibid.
7. Ibid.
8. Ibid., 199.
9. Ibid.

reconstruction of the past, in order to sustain the connections of the present and into the future, is a powerful reminder of how immigrants and their offspring must engage in this enterprise as well. Once again, Kreuger and Hanna build on the spiritual and psychological writings of Rollo May when they see the desire for understanding of one's past, "Whether an adoptee undertakes the actual physical act of searching or whether it remains a purely psychological longing, the desire itself can be seen as a natural aspect of each individual's struggle to reconcile fundamental concerns."[10]

> Our narrative is our identity. Within their stories, adoptees reveal perceptions and beliefs, internal working models of relationship, hopes and fantasies. Putting language and story to these fragmentary ideas reveals, both to the listener and to the self, what lies beneath. Once made conscious, it is then available for review, challenge and adjustment. Identity is the central mystery of adoption and there is no more fitting way to clarify identity than to bring to light the stories that underpin it.[11]

Biblical Narrative: Creation Accounts

The book of Genesis contains two narratives of the beginnings of our existence. While in captivity in Babylon, the Israelites' way of worshipping their God in the Promised Land was no longer viable; thus, they had to reach back to narratives of their origins that gave meaning to their existence in exile. It is from the need for the meaning of existence as individual and communal beings that narratives arise. Stories about our past bridge the gaps in our own memory as well as continuing an institutional memory for the entire group.

The beginning chapters reveal mystical stories of a cosmic nature, of how the world was created, and in particular, the creation of human beings in the image of God. Genesis chapters 1 and 2 contain differing accounts while depicting a similar rationale for

10. Ibid., 195; see also May, *Diversity of Being*, 1983.

11. Fitzhardinge, "Adoption," 67.

the creation of human beings by God. Neither account is unique to the Hebrew people as mythical tales about human conception and interaction with the divine were commonly dispersed in foreign regions. The purpose of utilizing these accounts for the Hebrew people was to fill in the "gaps" of their historical memory. Each account is attributed to different authors as they tell different ways the world and human beings were created. However, by changing the intention of God's creative act, the Hebrew people reconstructed a mystical narrative that revealed a monotheistic God in love with the creation called forth, especially the people created in the same divine image.

The Genesis accounts of creation were crafted by Hebrews who were in exile and took existing stories circulating in other cultures during their Babylonian captivity. The experience of being in exile, surrounded by a foreign culture and people in the Mesopotamia region contributed to the deeper understanding of the divine for the Hebrew people. In short, living away from what they had known in the Promised Land forced them to re-interpret the events of their history. Without direct knowledge or resources of the homeland, those in exile had to "re-create" their history utilizing stories that were readily available to them even if these stories were not part of their own oral tradition. By reinterpreting these stories in order to fill the gaps of the missing historical periods, the Israelites were able to continue their faith traditions while away from the land God had given them.

Although the two accounts of creation differ—partly because of the different writers involved, and partly because of the sources the authors had access to—they still contain within them similarities that held the Hebrew community together in maintaining the covenant. In particular, the first chapter of Genesis presents a systematic treatment of the creation of the world while the second chapter presents a more intimate encounter with God in a paradise-like garden setting. Both, however, illustrate the importance of a relationship with God, with one another and with creation as the central concern of the Hebrew faith life.

The encounter between Creator and creature is represented by human beings created in the image of God (Gen 1:27a) and having the Spirit of life breathed into them (Gen 2:7). These associations with the divine reveal a unique origin very different to their pagan counterparts. The purpose of creating humans differed as pagan customs reminded the people of the servile nature of their humanity in appeasing the gods, while the Hebrew accounts recognized the loving relationship God has called them into. Next, the communal nature of our beings is found in the creation of males and females. Within the creation of the world in six days, both men and women are created in the image of God (Gen 1:27b) and at the very end of creation. Being the pinnacle of God's creation, "it was very good" (Gen 1:31), the environment for humanity to thrive in was already in place as a sign of God's providential love and care. In the Garden of Eden, Adam is created first, but alone he is incomplete (Gen 2:18). Creating Eve from one of his ribs illustrates the relationships involved with every human encounter. Finally, human beings were created to be in relation with all of God's creation as good stewards. Entrustment of such responsibilities is revealed in the command of God for human beings to have dominion over creation (Gen 1:28). Dominion, here, is not about doing whatever one wishes to do, but rather, it is a task to care for creation as part of the relationship with God. Adam is also entrusted with a similar responsibility as he is asked by God to name all the animals (Gen 2:19). The act of naming connects Adam to creation in a bond symbolizing God's own work of creation. Naming makes something one's own and in the process, correlating responsibilities emerge.

The two stories of creation reveal the cosmic and mystical origins of our beings. Beyond just human origins, divine origins are just as important for those seeking to give meaning to their lives. Therefore, reasons for existence, rather than historical accuracy, are primary in remembering these narratives. In order to give a more complete meaning to one's *sitz im leben* or situation in life, the mystical accounts of our origin must also be complemented with historical figures illustrating the cosmic origins of our faith journey. For the Israelites, Abraham, the father of their faith, complements the creation accounts in Genesis by allowing the Hebrew people to trace their origins back within a specific ethnic faith group. The book of Genesis is not only about the beginnings of the Hebrew people as God's chosen, but a blueprint of sorts for those who choose to follow the same living God by embracing both a mystical or cosmic as well as human origin of their lives.

Biblical Narrative: The Call of Abraham

The LORD said to Abram: Go forth from your land, your relatives, and from your father's house to a land that I will show you. I will make of you a great nation, and I will bless you; I will make your name great, so that you will be a blessing. I will bless those who bless you and curse those who curse you. All the families of the earth will find blessing in you. Abram went as the LORD directed him, and Lot went with him. Abram was seventy-five years old when he left Haran. Abram took his wife Sarai, his brother's son Lot, all the possessions that they had accumulated, and the persons they had acquired in Haran, and they set out for the land of Canaan. (Gen 12:1–5 NAB)

The death, isolation, freedom, and meaningless that motivate adoptees to seek their past is also illustrated in Abraham's call to "go forth" in becoming the father of the faith. By being called out of his native land, these four elements emerge through his journey to another. The lack of possessions, especially for the protection of communal family, along with the insecurity of not possessing land reveal Abraham's vulnerability. God's promise is, then, only realized when Abraham embraces his new identity as the father of many, something that takes a lifetime to emerge. By being the first, Abraham models what future generations must do in re-creating a similar history in order to participate in the covenant with the one true God. Thus, one's own faith journey eventually finds its way back to Abraham's own loss of identity and the ways he was able to uncover his real identity in the living God. Abraham's journey away from his own people and birthplace is as much about the journey itself as it is about the new land to settle in, much like those who seek to recover their past in order to ground themselves in a meaningful reality today and into the future.

The search for a narrative in which to ground oneself by going beyond just the known world is a common theme found throughout the Old and New Testaments. In particular, the initial human encounter with the divine often involves a movement from the known to the unknown as characterized by Abraham and Sarah's journey. "In fact, it is Abraham's identity as [a nomadic foreigner] that directly facilitates the outworking of God's blessing given to Abraham in Genesis."[12] In the Old Testament, the formation of God's people begins with Abram and Sarai's call to become Abraham and Sarah in a new land. The call to leave one's existing family, communal relationships and homeland made Abraham and Sarah migrants of their own choosing. Their choice to leave their known world behind in search of a new grounding for their existence in the unknown meant that Abraham and Sarah would provide the narrative for future generations of believers to follow and uncover the real blessings of their lives just as they did.

The decision to leave their familiar environment represents a certain paradox as Abraham and Sarah no longer rely on their own abilities, living as members of a society with certain rights, but instead join the ranks of those who are living on the margins of society and having to relearn how to navigate through life with this emerging identity.[13] In addition, scripture is silent regarding Abraham's pedigree or why God would choose this individual over another. "It is thus that Abraham begins his entrance into literary fame as an unknown with no recorded personal achievements, no remarkable character traits, and no glorious past."[14] Thus, a notable reputation or pedigree is not the prerequisite for those exploring

12. Gallagher, "Abraham on the Move," 4.

13. Ibid., 7.

14. Ibid., 6.

the past to find meaning for the present. Rather, the search for significance in one's life is the only thing required by God.

Being a migrant is not an identity that easily fades, especially if the emerging identity is part of God's plan for bestowing a universal blessing. Abraham and Sarah's willingness to live as migrants requires a lifetime and even their offspring continue a similar existence. The fact that no land was acquired during Abraham and Sarah's lifetime for their resettlement and only in Sarah's death is Abraham able to acquire a burial land, highlights the fact that no home is truly established. Abraham's description of himself as a *ger* (גֵּר, Gen 23:4) or resident alien stresses his migrant status.[15] In addition, his descendants carry on this legacy as nomadic foreigners even though they are born in a place entirely different than their parents and would never return to that homeland.

> Various biblical texts call Israel's ancestors *gerim* (גֵּרִים, the plural form of *ger*) or describe their activities in the land as those of immigrants . . . Other biblical passages indicate that the people of Israel, the descendants of Abraham and Sarah, were also aliens or migrants, especially when they were slaves in Egypt and when they wandered in the wilderness.[16]

Abraham's status as a foreigner, a nomadic person, a migrant is further highlighted in his attempt to acquire a burial site for Sarah under the system of land rights then in place.[17] Abraham's status is revealed because he has no legal right to what the people hold most valuable and sacred—the land. "Abraham acknowledges that because of his low status as a resident sojourner he has no rights to land for burial."[18] However, the respect both parties involved have for one another legitimizes the transaction and in the end, allows Abraham to acquire the burial site for his wife. The land acquired must be used in a specific manner because of an implicit

15. Lenchak, "Israel's Ancestors," 20.

16. Ibid.

17. Stephen Russell utilizes the system of land rights from anthropologist Max Gluckman in Russell, "Abraham's Purchase."

18. Ibid., 170.

understanding of what the land being transferred is intended for.[19] Thus, the newly acquired land is intended for Sarah's burial and all their future descendants. It is interesting to note that because this land is intended for the dead, the living still do not have any home to call their own.

This realization that was afforded to Abraham and Sarah took their whole lifetime to materialize, further revealing God's patience with us. The covenant between God and Abraham, then, is more than the inheritance of a physical piece of property. Rather, it is found in the self-discovery that happens when settling down in another locale, which also eventually leads to the discovery of following God in an unprecedented manner.

Emerging identities resulting from one's inquiries into the past are a common theme throughout our faith journey. "Culture and ethnicity are central themes in scripture from Genesis to Revelation and play an integral part in God's plan for humanity."[20] Throughout salvation history, embracing death, isolation, freedom, and meaninglessness—factors that motivate us to scour our past for meaning—results in finding oneself as a new creation before God. The Korean American Catholic experience of faith engages many of these biblical themes, especially the call to "go forth," in order for the cultural experiences of this group to further develop. Too often, faith in Korean American communities is not presented as something constitutive of the culture or the cultural aspect as constitutive to the faith expression. Both are necessary elements since faith and culture are intertwined in the lives of Korean American Catholics.

Korean Narrative: Gojoseon Kingdom

Most cultural faith groups embrace both a historical as well as a mythical or cosmic narrative; likewise, Korean Catholics can trace their existence from stories from both heavenly and earthly realms

19. Ibid., 162.

20. Gringrich and Smith, "Culture and Ethnicity," 140.

as well. The legendary story explaining the existence of the Korean people is based on a deity coming down from heaven and establishing a particular race prior to modern Korean history.

> Once upon a time, there was *Hwanin*. His son *Hwanung* was born from a concubine. He often expressed his desire to come down from heaven to earth to live among humans . . . And *Hwanin* thought he would be of benefit to mankind; thereupon gave his son three talismans and sent him on his way to rule . . . He had power over the lords of the winds, the rains, and the clouds. And he also commanded decisions over the planting of grains, human life, disease, punishments, and the determining of good and evil.[21]

Besides descending to the level of humanity, the significance of Hwanung is seen in his encounter with a tiger and a bear desiring to become human. In order to become human, Hwanung instructs both creatures to consume twenty cloves of garlic and mugwort for their dietary needs while staying out of the sun for a hundred days. As the legend goes, the tiger quickly grew impatient and gave up on becoming human. However, the bear endured the dietary restrictions and emerged from the dark as a female human being. Desiring also motherhood, she now prayed for a child. Eventually, her prayers were answered as she conceived a son, Dangun.

The legend of Dangun is not only about the kingdom that was established on earth, the beginning of the Korean people, but also how Koreans are connected to the heavenly realm. Unlike the Genesis accounts which begin with the creation of the world, this narrative speaks more of the connection between the heavenly and earthly realms through a dynastic lineage of a certain group of people. "Historians trace the birth of Korean nationalist historiography to the theorists and leaders of the anti-Japanese independence movement, whose goals were aimed at raising the national consciousness of the Korean people."[22] Therefore, the cosmic beginnings of the Korean people were told by the inhabitants

21. Pai, *Constructing "Korean" Origins*, 61.

22. Ibid., 7.

to instill a worthwhile legacy for a people searching for identity in the aftermath of the Korean War and in purging the Japanese influences on the Korean peninsula.[23]

The legend of Dangun holds a certain place in Korean society. The legend continues to serve many purposes as the dynamics of the Korean people are rapidly transforming in a global world. The mythical tales of Dangun became popular especially during the Japanese occupation of Korea since it was the Korean people's way of preserving their identity as something other than that of their oppressors. By acknowledging Dangun, who was both human and divine, as their founder, the people of the Korean peninsula could now appeal to a time that existed prior to any foreign occupation as well as encompassing a territory much greater than the current state of both South and North Korea combined.

> Gojoseon, Korea's first state, and its ruler Dangun have been recognized as national autonomy and mobility for a long time. The Dangun myth is recorded in *Samguk yusa* (Memorabilia of the Three Kingdoms) and *Jewangun-gi* (Songs of Emperors and Kings), and there has been much research and discussion on their historical characters. In particular, when Korea became a Japanese colony, nationalist historians and Daejonggyo (a native religion in Korea that believes Dangun is its founder) accelerated a national movement about Dangun and Gojoseon.[24]

When Koreans were trying to emerge from the ashes of poverty and war, such storytelling seemed unnecessary and foolish. Following the examples of the West, the entire country in the southern peninsula sought a better life by mimicking a path of educational success which would also eventually lead to economic and political success. Those who followed such a path instilled by the Western mindset also had little need for such legendary stories. However, with the success of Korea's global economy, the legend of Dangun is now retold for different reasons. The mythical story that seemed unscientific and unrealistic when the country was

23. Ibid., 1.
24. Paek, "Descriptions," 213.

underdeveloped, is now a legend used to distinguish the importance of Korea and the people who have emerged today in the Far East.[25] The adherence to this legend has many ramifications as it serves to create a national identity that is unique to all other Asians in the region. In addition, by tracing their lineage to a prehistoric history, Koreans also expand their presence geographically, as Dangun's father emerged on the mountain known as Baekdusan near the border of North Korea and China.

> An important aspect of Baekdusan's imagined geographies is its mythological component. Myth not only has the power to ingrain, through its aura of sacredness, certain sorts of images upon the myth's protagonist or the places in which the myth takes place, but also can imprint, upon the audience, imagined images, as produced through the processes of interpreting and introducing myths . . . It is worth considering if such "geographical exteriority" increased psychological intimacy. A sense of origin as well as desire to recover the "lost" territory may have contributed in creating a certain sort of image of that place.[26]

The imagination that this expansion captures, allows Koreans to trace their history beyond just the northern regions of the Korean peninsula as speculations of Korean influence also reach to farther ends of the then known world.[27]

This mythical origin of the Korean people is useful in uniting the Korean people based on race, language, territory, history, religion, and customs.[28] The legend of Dangun appeals to the Korean psyche because of its emphasis on factors of unification based on a notion of ethnic purity. By claiming the origination of their heritage in prehistoric moments, Koreans are able to conceive of themselves as a singular homogenous racial group descending

---

25. Andronova and Abrosimova, "Mythologizing History."

26. Cho, "The Significance of Perceptions," 34–35.

27. Andronova and Abrosimova, "Mythologizing History," 602–3.

28. Pai, *Constructing "Korean" Origins*, 57; see also Hang-gu Kim, "An Analysis of the Contents," 29–53.

from their initial ancestor, Dangun, on the sacred mountaintop of Baekdusan.[29] Just as the Garden of Eden served to symbolize a time and place where all creation was in harmony with God, Baekdusan also symbolizes the sacred homeland for both South and North Koreans. Therefore, Dangun has emerged as a historical figure in Korean textbooks and in the institutional memory as someone who actually lived around the Bronze Age (1000 BC) or even as early as the Neolithic period (3000 BC).[30]

The clinging to such mythical origins parallels the way the Hebrew people formulated and circulated the creation narratives while in exile. The Israelites and the Korean people were oppressed and during these periods of being dominated, both sought a way to preserve their identities by appealing to heavenly origins to expand the horizons they were captive in. Contained in these legendary sources are elements of truths of an entire people that the oppressors tried to destroy or at least scorn as inferior. The recounting of these narratives allowed both groups to endure their conditions and one day proudly proclaim their heritage during oppressive moments as well as being utilized afterwards. In many ways, these stories of origin filled the gaps when the institutional memory was lost or incomplete.

Korean Catholic Narrative:
Martyr of Blood & Martyr of Sweat

Just as the Hebrew people trace their faith lineage back to a specific historical figure in the person of Abraham, other ethnic faith groups who follow Christ are invited to do the same. As Catholics, we must also trace our heritage through the rich litany of saints—other "Abrahamic figures of the faith" within our own heritage—while tracing our lineage back to Abraham. Those men and women who trusted God in a similar manner and sacrificed for the future of the church must also be part of the historical

29. Ibid., 57–58.

30. Ibid., 60; see also Yi, *A New History of Korea*; and Kim, *The Origins of the Korean Race*.

memory contributing to the identity of an ethnic people of faith. People who endured similar occasions of death, isolation, meaninglessness and freedom need to be acknowledged in gratitude for their service to the community along with their measure of commitment to the faith.

There are now 227 Korean martyrs officially recognized by the Catholic Church, with the beatification of 124 martyrs by Pope Francis in 2014, and over 8,000 who gave their lives for the faith whose names are unknown; therefore, there are plenty of historic figures Koreans could use to create a cultural Catholic lineage. From official saints to those yet to be canonized, foreign and native clergy, male and female laity, young and old alike, Koreans have a multitude of saintly and "Abrahamic" figures to draw upon as their origins and inspiration of the faith. Two figures for Korean Catholics stand out, Andrew Taegon Kim and Thomas Yang Eop Choe. St. Andrew Taegun Kim was canonized as part of the 103 Korean Martyrs in 1984 during Pope John Paul II's visit to that country while Thomas Yang Eop Choe is still awaiting official recognition from the universal church although many revere him in Korea.

Andrew Taegon Kim was ordained in 1845, the first native Korean priest. His priestly ministry lasted only a short duration with his martyrdom in 1846; thus his taking on the title, "martyr of blood." His death by beheading was no different than the tragic death that many others suffered for the faith during the persecutions against Catholics that lasted until 1866. In contrast, Thomas Yang Eop Choe, the second native priest of Korea, did not die a martyr's death but a "natural" one due to typhoid in 1861. Soon after his ordination in 1849, Thomas Yang Eop Choe became known as the "martyr of sweat" because of his unrelenting efforts to nurture the nascent communities of faith. His pastoral work consisted of walking over 1,700 miles a year to administer the necessary sacraments as Catholics were being persecuted throughout the countryside.

The dichotomy presented by Andrew Taegon Kim and Thomas Yang Eop Choe is a serious matter in the church today and in our attempts to trace our cultural faith heritage. All Asian saints, that I can recall, are martyrs (e.g., Korean martyrs, Filipino martyrs, Vietnamese martyrs, Japanese martyrs, etc.) with none being canonized for their holiness demonstrated throughout their lives. This "one-sidedness" naturally skews the recovery of one's faith heritage. While the martyrs are worthy examples of how to follow Christ, they constitute only a specific segment of the entire church's population. In addition, martyrs during the 19th century are remembered because their names were recorded as part of the wealthy, educated or royal class. Although 227 Korean martyrs are officially sanctioned, the over 8,000 or so nameless will never be recognized in the same manner because their identities were never recorded. Therefore, the martyrs, while they should be revered in our faith tradition for their sacrifice, are not enough to complete the picture for those seeking deeper meaning from their origins of faith. The difference here between Abraham and Andrew Kim is that we are aware of the faults and failures of such a patriarch in his attempt to live out a faithful life of following God. St. Andrew, on the other hand, does not provide us with important narratives of both failures and successes to imitate, other than the link from his martyrdom to the universal church.

Perhaps it is the lack of information about St. Andrew Kim that appeals to the Korean psyche. Similar to the mythical legend of the origination of the Korean people, the early martyrdom of St. Andrew Kim allows Koreans to shape their storytelling. Just as the Dangun narrative was used to solidify a Korean identity, the martyrs also afford similar opportunities in terms of a religious one. The upholding of the Korean martyrs epitomizes the growth of the Korean Catholic Church through a spirit of innovation and sacrifice. The spirit of innovation is revealed in the origins of the Catholic faith in Korea. Rather than through direct missionary activities, the laity encountered the faith in China and evangelized others in Korea as they created communities of faith before any clergy or missionary personnel arrived on the Korean peninsula. The spirit of sacrifice is demonstrated by the seeds of the faith that were planted through the blood of the martyrs, as Catholics worshipped only the one true God and not their ancestors. Therefore, the martyrdom of St. Andrew Kim and others who also died for the faith illustrates the innovation and sacrifice that allowed not only the country of Korea to emerge from the ashes of poverty and war, but also the Catholic Church to be a prime example of the faith for Asia and other parts of the world. In addition, other recent achievements in the church such as the growing numbers of vocations and laity are now attributed to the selfless acts of the ones who originally paved the way. Although many lost their lives on behalf of the faith during several periods of persecution, the first native clergy still stands out, symbolizing the way Koreans want to remember their past, by overcoming their tragedies through innovative ways and reaping the rewards of their sacrifice.

An Emerging Korean American Catholic Narrative

Similar to the creation stories found in the Old Testament and in the legendary tale of Dangun, Korean American Catholics are also able to attribute their origins or connections to the homeland through divine intervention in both church and society, thereby creating a heavenly or cosmic account for their being. However, this narrative differs from previous stories of origination by the simple fact that the Korean American Catholic narrative is not told with an appropriated meaning shaped by the storyteller in a mythical manner. Rather, the Korean American Catholic narrative involving the movement of the Holy Spirit both in church and the world is a historical reality to be uncovered and treasured.

The emergence of a cultural people of faith in the United States would not have happened without the Spirit's movement in the church opening her doors to the world through the Second Vatican Council (1962–1965) and the United States opening her shores to immigrants from all over the world through the Immigration and Naturalization Act of 1965 (a.k.a. Hart-Celler Act). Thus, Koreans, almost unknowingly, embraced their immigrant journey by carrying with them a cultural heritage along with the faith of the martyrs. Over 50 million people live in South Korea while 1.7 million Korean Americans were reported as living in the

United States in the 2010 Census. Since the majority of Christians in South Korea are Protestants, one would assume that those in the United States would then follow a similar pattern. In fact, a greater percentage of Korean immigrants in the United States profess a Protestant affiliation. Approximately 60% of Korean Americans belong to a Protestant denomination compared to roughly 15% in the homeland; whereas, Korean Catholics and their immigrant counterparts are a little over 10% of the total population. Various reasons explain why an overwhelming portion of Korean immigrants subscribes to the Protestant faith. These range from extensive social services offered by religious institutions to greater congregational numbers providing numerous religious ministries and social activities. Over the past couple of decades there has been a trend growing among the next generation of Korean American Protestants toward creating a religious "third space" of their own by either starting a new generational community among themselves, by joining other Asian groups and creating a Pan-Asian worship space, or becoming a fully multiracial faith community.[31]

Whereas the Protestant faith struggles to emphasize a cultural aspect of Christianity as illustrated by the next generation, the Catholic faith necessitates the reception of a cultural heritage in order to deepen the understanding of the faith and make it relevant for each generation. The role of tradition in the Catholic faith requires cultural understanding for its ongoing transmission. This was one of the great developments at the Second Vatican Council as it allowed the church to engage the world. Without a cultural context, the universal message of God's love would not impact the hearts and minds of the believers. This task of preserving the culture within the religious sphere is what distinguishes Catholics, especially those in the immigrant's situation. Maintaining this cultural sensitivity is also what makes the Korean American Catholic existence a continuation of God's calling for a migrant church as an ongoing revelation of Pentecost in the world.

The Second Vatican Council changed the relationship between the church and the world when Pope John XXIII called for

31. Kim, *A Faith of Our Own*, 133.

the twenty-first ecumenical council shortly after his election as Holy Pontiff on January 25, 1959. Previously, such gatherings of church leaders formed when there were either doctrinal disputes or other church matters that threatened the unity of the faith. Despite the healthy status of churches in Europe and North America, the "good pope"—as John XXIII is fondly referred to—saw the need for internal and external renewals in his prophetic understanding of the church's engagement with society. Even with the unexpected invocation for the council and without fully understanding the procedures or ramifications from such a gathering, the council fathers came together, unified by this call for renewal.

From the turn of the twentieth century, Koreans have been immigrating to the United States for a variety of reasons. Early on, Koreans sought asylum as political refugees or to accompany migrant workers as picture brides, matched solely at the discretion of the matchmaker based on one's photo. Although immigration from Korea to the United States is categorized within three periods (1903–45, 1945–65, post–1965), the usage of the term "Korean American" mainly applies to the third period known as the post–1965 immigration wave. A number of factors contribute to the exclusion of other immigrant generations when speaking of Korean Americans, including the lack of any substantial numbers of immigrants to be noticed by society, the desire of political refugees to return to Korea, and the lack of any structural legacies in the early resettlement stages. In addition, the immigrants themselves needed time for maturation in order to begin reconciling the cultural identities of their homeland with their host country. Thus, only in the post–1965 immigration era does the term "Korean American" really apply based on several factors, all of which contribute to mystical and historic narratives.

Prior to legislative reform in 1965, immigrants from only a handful of European countries were welcomed to this country. All others were placed on a biased quota system that restricted foreigners rather than welcoming them. The Immigration and Naturalization Act of 1965 changed the immigration landscape by placing family reunification as the top priority for immigration.

Therefore, the Korean American narrative revolves around this immigration reform but must also acknowledge the groundwork that was forged before the passage of the legislative act. Being able to identify these developments in the United States as part of the workings of the Holy Spirit is what makes this a cosmic narrative for Korean Americans as well as all immigrants affected by the 1965 legislation.

The connection between the Civil Rights Movement and the change in the US immigration policy in the 60s is quite simple—without the activities of the Civil Rights Movement and the passage of the Civil Rights Act in 1964, the Immigration and Nationality Act of 1965 may not have been established within the timeframe that it was. Without the call for equality regardless of ethnicity represented in the Civil Rights Movement, the opening of doors to immigrants from such diverse ethnic backgrounds would have been unfathomable. The 1965 US Immigration Act lifted the prejudicial exclusion laws of immigrants in general, and Asians in particular, by allowing families to come to the United States and create a new life in a country originally founded on this model of immigration.

The Immigration and Nationality Act of 1965 was not as dramatic for the entire nation, as changes to the immigration policy came as a result of the Civil Rights Movement, furthering the cause of obtaining people's civil rights by going beyond just desegregation. Thanks to the struggles of the Black community, the rest of world also reaped the benefits of racial equality and could see the overall movement for justice as part of God's economy. However, one would be hard pressed to find anyone who immigrated during the post–1965 wave to consider the activities of the Spirit and their new beginnings in this country as having a cosmic origin or being divinely inspired. In fact, the immigration revisions twenty-five years later would dampen any such mystical outlook as well.

In addition to legislative changes for equality, Asians themselves needed to reflect on their own struggles for social acceptance. Building on the momentum of the Civil Rights Movement, students of Asian descent rallied on college campuses and began to empower their communities with similar ideals. One result of this movement was the naming of this ethnic group as Asian Americans rather than the former, pejorative, Orientals. This emergence of an identity that is similar to that in one's homeland, yet which acknowledges the complexities of identity formation as immigrants was needed in addition to the overall changes in church and society.

Fifty years after the passage of the Hart-Celler Act, divisions within immigrant groups are now apparent. The context for immigration for Koreans of the 70s and 80s is vastly different from that of those who come to the United States in the new millennium with the rapid development of Korea as a whole. Although history has shown that countries of emigration may eventually rise out of poverty or overcome their desperate conditions over time, recovery usually takes generations to occur. For example, certain European immigrants such as the Irish or Polish began immigrating to the US as early as the 1800s and some of these countries of origin needed several generations to rise out of their economic and political situation. In the case of South Korea, within one generation, this tiny country, only slightly larger than the state of Indiana and smaller than Kentucky, has made its focus on education pay off by becoming a global competitor in many economic fields. While European immigrants justified their reasons for departure since their home country underwent recovery for generations, Korean immigrants and their offspring began questioning if their reasons for departure were truly valid after the rapid development of their homeland. Thus, the developments of the homeland as well as the status of the initial immigrants make it difficult to see the origination of Korean Americans as inspired by the Holy Spirit and as a heavenly narrative.

Korean American Catholics are now reaching a milestone as they approach their golden jubilee of being officially recognized by both church and society. While the 1965 US Immigration Act welcomed people from around the world, especially those in difficult circumstances derived from poverty and war, the US Catholic Church also responded by welcoming these cultural groups as part of their overall community in 1966. This recognition does not suggest that liturgical gatherings did not exist in various pockets of society throughout the United States prior to this recognition. Rather, it signifies the response of both church and society to the Holy Spirit through the official recognition and inclusion of Korean American Catholics into the US ecclesial structures. Therefore in 2016, Korean American Catholics will celebrate 50 years of their established cultural and religious heritage in the United States.

The Korean American Catholic experience reached a pivotal moment in 1966 when the Archdiocese of San Francisco acknowledged the growing commitment of Korean immigrants in their neighborhoods by establishing the first officially recognized Korean American Catholic community at St. Michael's.[32] Although several communities existed throughout the United States prior to this declaration, the official sanctioning by a diocese meant that Korean Americans were now officially part of the US religious landscape. This milestone of being officially recognized is important today because it is truly the "starting point" for Catholics of Korean descent. In other words, the ability to create an identity by reflecting on what it means to be Korean American Catholic would not have been possible without the cultural, social, and religious space afforded at this time.

This golden jubilee is also a culmination of the cultural and religious experience stemming from the emergence of the Catholic faith on the Korean peninsula over a century ago and in this country after the 1965 US Immigration Act and the Second Vatican Council. With this new status as members of an ecclesial community, Korean American Catholics were allowed to begin expressing their spiritual needs: in particular, the lack of priestly leadership in their midst. This sacramental void within the immigrant community resembled the nascent faith community on the Korean peninsula in the 18th century. Through the support of the universal church, in particular, missioners from China and then France, the faithful in Korea laid the foundation for future generations of

32. Peace Times Weekly, "The Formation of Catholic Community in the Mid-60s," 1.

believers on the Korean peninsula. Similarly, through the support of the universal church, especially the welcoming clergy and faith communities in the US, Korean American Catholics were given the opportunity to begin forging their cultural religious identity. However, the necessary emergence of "Abrahamic figures" has not materialized in the immigration process.

Although this anniversary will recall past contributions, this commemoration will more importantly celebrate present realities since without this focus, Korean American Catholics cannot continue to grow into the future as significant contributors to both Church and society. In order to move forward as a unique people of faith gleaning the richness from both countries of origin and destination, Korean American Catholics must not only respect their past, but equally important, honor their current struggles as well as their achievements. The early martyrs embraced their situation by offering their lives; today's descendants in the United States continue to do so by honoring their displaced situations by sacrificing for future generations. The early community forged a new identity as Catholics on the Korean peninsula; similarly, Korean American Catholics must also allow a new cultural religious identity to emerge from their experience of migration and faith, especially in raising "Abrahamic figures" linking Korean American Catholics to the faith of their homeland as well as the faith found in the scriptures. In truth, Korean American Catholics do not garner the same acclaim of their Korean counterparts, and without such acknowledgment the future is difficult to embrace with the hope that is afforded us in faith. Therefore, this commemoration is a remembrance of the connections of our faith and also a powerful reminder of the lack of a Korean American Catholic narrative that traces this faith group's lineage through specific figures found in the immigrant faith journey.

Conclusion

The importance of origin is critical for human development and particularly so for Korean descendants, illustrated by the association to a *gohyang* or hometown. This place of origin, the *gohyang*, naturally connects people to the past as well as with one another in present day encounters. Being associated with a particular *gohyang* creates a familial environment regardless of blood ties. These hometowns serve a multitude of purposes in the lives of Koreans; in particular, the connection to one's place of origin also becomes one's connection to ancestral roots as well as always maintaining a home at least in the heart and mind of the individual. In the past, one's *gohyang* also served as an important reminder of the need to return back home, as those who journeyed far away longed for the time of their return. Korean American Catholics' lack of identification with a *gohyang* is reflective of their lack of narratives of who they are.

Similar to many nonadoptees, Korean Americans have taken their history for granted and the search for their origins or specific connections to the past following the immigration process has not been properly undertaken. Because the history of Korean immigrants and their offspring has not been closely examined or questioned, many living in the United States as Korean descendants do not truly understand their origins as an ethnic group and also the importance of their cultural faith heritage. The uncovering of one's past is not only difficult, but it is also a painful process at times, especially when it directly involves further confusion about ourselves before any clarity can be achieved. The linguistic and cultural challenges alone can quickly discourage anyone, let alone the scant resources about the departure from Korea and resettlement in the United States.

Both the desire to search for one's origins as adoptees and the assumed history of nonadoptees are evident in the Korean American Catholic immigration experience. The lack of concern exposes the ambivalence that immigrants and their offspring have in approaching their historical memory. Often, the initial immigrants are hard at work providing for their families and have neither the luxury for such a reflection nor the desire for it. Slowly, through later generations, the stories are recovered and valued as part of the historical memory. The desire to find one's origins also helps us in realizing that every immigrant faith community must comb the past in order to understand its future. Korean Americans now have the resources and abilities to do so after 50 years of maturation. Regardless of whether one is adopted or not, professes a Christian faith or another belief, is an initial immigrant or of a subsequent generation, the recovery of stories that are both historic and mythical in nature, is a constitutive aspect of understanding one's place in the world.

In particular, Korean immigrants and their offspring assume a natural flow of their historical narrative without realizing the rupture that often takes place in displacement and resettlement in the immigration process. Any attempts to explain our current existence will be incomplete and the missing gaps of this historical recollection are part of the mystery that fuels our faith. Therefore, the search for our origins also reveals that our past includes elements of both earthly and heavenly mysteries as passed down through a communal memory. In other words, understanding where we came from is more than merely discovering data and facts about ourselves. Rather, this search for identity often leads to the discovery of our individual beings intertwined within the entire fabric of humanity. In short, to discover our Catholic identity is to discover our cultural identity of being Korean American and vice versa.

Bibliography

Andronova, Larisa, and Ekaterina Abrosimova. "Mythologizing History in South Korea." *Procedia: Social and Behavioral Sciences* 166 (2015) 601–4.

Brodzinsky, David M., et al. *Being Adopted: The Lifelong Search for Self.* New York: Anchor, 1993.

Cho, Hyun-soul. "The Significance of Perceptions of Baekdusan in Baekdu-related Myths." *The Review of Korean Studies* 13, no. 4 (2010) 33–52.

Darongkamas, Jurai, and Louise Lorenc. "Going Back to Our Roots." *The Psychologist* 21, no. 12 (2008) 1022–25.

Fitzhardinge, Helen. "Adoption, Resilience and the Importance of Stories: The Making of a Film about Teenage Adoptees." *Adoption & Fostering* 32, no. 1 (2008) 58–68.

Fitzmyer, Joseph. *Romans.* Anchor Yale Bible Commentaries. New Haven, VT: Yale University Press, 2007.

Gallagher, Sarita. "Abraham on the Move: The Outpouring of God's Blessing through a Migrant." In *God's People on the Move: Biblical and Global Perspectives on Migration and Mission,* edited by vanThanh Nguyen and John M. Prior, 3–17. Eugene, OR: Wipf & Stock, 2014.

Gaillardetz, Richard. "The Church as Sacrament: Towards an Ecclesial Spirituality." *The Way: Supplement* (1999) 22–34.

Gringrich, Fred, and Bradford Smith. "Culture and Ethnicity in Christianity/Psychology Integration: Review and Future Directions." *Journal of Psychology and Christianity* 33, no. 2 (2014) 139–55.

Kim, Sharon. *A Faith of Our Own: Second-Generation Spirituality in Korean American Churches.* Piscataway, NJ: Rutgers University Press, 2010.

Kim, Simon C. *Harmony in Faith: Korean American Catholics.* Washington, DC: USCCB, 2015.

———. *Memory and Honor: Cultural and Generational Ministry with Korean American Communities.* Collegeville, MN: Liturgical, 2013.

Kim, Sook Hyun, and Pyong Gap Min. "The Post-1965 Korean Immigrants: Their Characteristics and Settlement Patterns." *Korea Journal of Population and Development* 21, no. 2 (1992) 121–43.

King, Martin Luther, Jr. *Why We Can't Wait.* Boston: Beacon, 2011.

Kreuger, Mary Jago, and Fred Hanna. "Why Adoptees Search: An Existential Treatment Perspective." *Journal of Counseling and Development* 75:3 (1997) 195–202.

Lenchak, Timothy. "Israel's Ancestors as Gerim: A Lesson of Biblical Hospitality." In *God's People on the Move: Biblical and Global Perspectives on Migration and Mission,* 18–28. Eugene, OR: Wipf & Stock, 2014.

Min, Pyong Gap. *Koreans in North America: Their Twenty-First Century Experiences.* Lanham: Lexington, 2013.

Paek, Chang Ki. "Descriptions of the History of Gojoseon Shown in Foreign Textbooks." *The Review of Korean Studies* 10, no. 4 (2007) 211–28.

Pai, Hyung Il. *Constructing "Korean" Origins: A Critical Review of Archaeology, Historiography, and Racial Myth in Korean State-Formation Theories.* Cambridge: Harvard University Asia Center, 2000.

Peace Times Weekly. "The Formation of Catholic Community in the Mid-60s." *Peace Times Weekly* 710 (2003) 1.

Russell, Stephen C. "Abraham's Purchase of Ephron's Land." *Biblical Interpretation* 21, no. 2 (2013) 153–70.

2

The Korean American Catholic
Experience as Part of an Ongoing
Pentecost

 Paul D. Lee

THE VERY DEFINITION OF Pentecost exudes "outwardliness." To go forth, to go out into the world, to engage humanity, embodies the spirit of the Pentecost. Such a spirit also underscores the very catholicity of our faith. In this orchestra of universality, Korean American Catholics can play an instrumental role in advancing and celebrating the Pentecost. Korean American Catholics are uniquely positioned today to meet this challenge.

The US Catholic Church is becoming increasingly multicultural through continuing migration. In our Catholic community, this had led to the phenomenon of shared parishes. My last three parishes in the Washington metropolitan area have included cultural groups such as a Croatian mission, a Korean community, a Filipino community, a Latin American community, etc. I have tried to be hospitable and amenable to each group, cognizant of their experiences, fears and dreams as immigrants, as members of a non-mainstream group. My current parish boasts over sixty nationalities. Reflecting this kaleidoscope of nationality, I instituted a monthly intercultural Mass. Rather than naming it "multicultural," I sought to emphasize the "inter"–cultural aspect of our common existence. Being multicultural designates the status quo, but being intercultural points to where we want to go and what we want to become as a faith community regardless of our ethnicity. Reaching out to one another is to practice the catholicity of our faith. That is, thinking and acting according to a totality of the whole, centered around Christ. A parish is a school of communion and the Holy Spirit shows us the way.

The Holy Spirit constitutes the Church ever anew, which remains provisional and proleptic. This state of "temporariness" resonates with Korean American Catholics in their current transient status. Jesus envisions a new human family regardless of ethnic, religious, gender or linguistic lines. Paul speaks of Christ who "reconciles everything in his person" (Col 1:20), "one new man" and proclaims "All are one Christ Jesus" (Gal 3:28). In the Incarnation, Jesus crosses the border between the divine and human, between the eternal and the temporal. Border crossing is most clear in the Pentecost event.[1] The Holy Spirit offers an eschatological hope to be experienced and realized now. The Holy Spirit provides a new meeting ground for dialogue with and exchange between various cultural groups.[2] There are cultural and spiritual elements and ethos that are peculiar and distinct to Korean American Catholics and at the same time salient enough to be able to contribute to the common good of the Church universal. Unfortunately, Korean American Catholics have been monocultural or bicultural at best. Korean American Catholics must move beyond an entrenchment mentality in isolation. It is the challenge of modern times for Korean American Catholics to actively live out the catholicity of the faith.

---

1. Stelzer, "New Ecclesial Reality," 15.

2. Lee, *Pneumatological Ecclesiology*, 277–78.

Korean Americans on the Move

The immigrant experience is not uniquely Korean. All immigrants are likely to carry a sense of cosmic loneliness, feeling all alone in the universe. The immigrant as a person on the move is likely to have an acute sense of displacement, uprootedness, poverty, lost/confused identity, vulnerability, and alienation. Thus, in a way, the "transient" trait of the immigrant's experience is similar to the temporariness of the Church on the move (*Ecclesia in via*). Most pertinently, the immigrant is suspended between two worlds, belonging to dual cultures, subject to dual alienation as he is neither fully integrated into nor fully accepted by two different cultural systems.

But the Korean immigrant experience is unique precisely because of its relative "success." Though Korean American life stories are remarkably diverse, many Korean immigrants are subjected to caricatures, myths, and misconceptions, be they complimentary or derogatory. Because of the reputation of being a 'model minority' for achieving financial and educational success, Koreans are also perceived as greedy, gun-happy, rude and crude, and exploitative of Blacks. "Success" also obscures the "unsuccessful" stories, of which there are many. Underneath the surface of Ivy League students and financial achievements lies the vast majority of Korean immigrants who are unemployed, underemployed, and uneducated. And all Korean immigrants, regardless of status or income, have experienced what it feels like to be perpetual foreigners or outsiders.[3] The elites among Korean immigrants who have made some traction in upward mobility seek to gain some political influence. But unfortunately, these elites focus on their own influence in society writ large rather than organizing their fellow Koreans to advance as a group for better welfare and needs. The number of Korean American associations is mind-numbingly large. Despite the proliferation of such associations, they rarely work together or join forces to pose a large and unified front.

3. Min, "Literature Review," 21.

Thus, the role of the Church for Korean American immigrants looms even larger. While, to many cultural Catholics, the church may be just a historical inheritance and family heritage, the community of faith is central to the actual experience of being Korean American. Over 70% of Korean Americans have an affiliation with Korean ethnic churches. Over 80% of the church-affiliated attend church once a week or more. The church for Korean Americans is therefore a safe haven for cultural identity and social interaction, operating as an extended family. The church provides a means of continuity with the past through reaffirmation of traditional values and coping with the problems of the present. Even if the value of religion is usually considered in spiritual terms, for many immigrants there are many social and economic benefits from participation in religious organizations. The church becomes an ethnic, cultural, social, and spiritual home for most immigrants. This explains their active involvement and heightened anticipation in the life of the church. The church also satisfies the need for social recognition especially when there is little to no recognition for individuals in their adopted society.

Beyond serving as a cultural and social safe haven, there is a critical need for Korean American Catholics to stand in the front line of a radically new human community centered around Christ. Pope Francis has said that the church is a healer—a field hospital after a battle—and a reconciler representing the sign and instrument of unity for the life of the world. The church has to re-examine its vision and goal, renew its commitment to the gospel, and respond to the conditions of the people with the heart of the Good Shepherd. This involves reimagining a new way of being a church of Pentecost.

Maturation and Growth

The Holy Spirit is the go-between between God and man, and shows the way forward for the church. Korean American Catholics, as an "in-between people" can bridge, relate, connect, reconcile, heal and unite the bond of love between fellow human beings.

The Holy Spirit shows the way. In the absence of the Holy Spirit, the church is just an assembly of human beings. With the Holy Spirit, the church is convoked to be like a sacrament of Christ for the life of the world. "The Spirit is communion (*koinonia*), sharing, participation, fellowship in the Trinitarian life (2 Cor 13:13; 1 John 1:1–10; 3:23–24). Without the mission of the Spirit there is neither communion with God nor communion among believers."[4] The Church then would be filled with people but devoid of meaning, and existentially empty.

But with the Holy Spirit the church is heaven on earth, the communion with the Divine Persons and with one another. Thus, the church exists only through ongoing epiclesis. John Taylor says: "You cannot commune with the Holy Spirit, for he *is* communion itself . . . Remember the strange familiarity of the skin-diver's casually brushing contact with the marine life around him. In such a way the Holy Spirit brings us into more vivid contact with one another and with God while remaining imperceptible himself."[5] That is why we say the Spirit is about *how*, while Christ is about *what*. Christ reveals the full glory of heaven, while the Spirit helps us to experience it on earth. It is the Holy Spirit that consoles the brokenhearted, that unites and reconciles all. Thus, holding fruitful and open dialogue with other Christian branches and other religions is to imitate God who initiates and continues the dialogue of salvation.

Korean American Catholics can work as that bridge, inspired by the Holy Spirit. The Korean American Catholic communities have long suffered the lack of proper pastoral leadership for their specific pastoral context, while the laity languished as spiritual orphans, sheep without a shepherd. The problems are multifaceted. Many priests serving Korean American Catholic communities often arrive here unprepared with hardly any idea of where they were sent or what they are supposed to accomplish.

The Korean American Priests Association (KAPA) in recent years has been a bridge and healer for many priests and

4. McDonnell, *Other Hand of God*, 228.

5. Taylor, *Go-Between God*, 43–44.

communities through orientation programs for the newly arrived pastoral ministers and by mediating between the diocese and the priest/community, by attempting conflict resolution in some communities, by offering scripturally based visions for healing and reconciliation such as the salutary story of Joseph in Genesis, and by mediating between the Korean bishops conference and the US bishops conference.

Likewise, Korean American Catholics can be the bridge. For Korean American Catholics, it is not so much about *what* but about *how* that is critical. Past mistakes and missteps can be remedied. They know that they are called to befriend and imitate Christ, and it is the Holy Spirit who shows how. The church has essentially served as a field hospital and rehab center for Korean American Catholics. Now the church needs to be the training ground of communion, encountering Christ, exercising the love of neighbor and being a healer of divisions and conflicts.

Vision and Direction

The Spirit blows as the wind does. Therefore, we must be acutely attentive to the signs of the times. We must be proactive in following the lead of the Spirit. Being proactive means that one must seek a vision beyond national parishes by establishing intercultural parishes, a new pastoral, spiritual, and theological challenge. Recognizing diversity, exercising hospitality, sharing resources, and collaborating in parish strategic planning are necessary in working towards this Catholic unity.

The current phenomenon of broadening the definition and mission of American culture and church is another sign of the times. Korean American Catholics broaden the definition of what it means to be an ethnic people embracing a cultural faith, thereby refusing to be trapped by opposing identities. Korean American Catholics are peculiarly strong and insistent in establishing their own faith communities throughout the United States (unlike other groups, e.g., French or Filipino communities), something which is a vital contribution to the overall ecclesial mission of evangelization. Korean American Catholics manifest their entrepreneurship, taking initiatives, especially among lay people. Korean American Catholics also are adept at forming dynamic small communities in every parish, bursting with energy, enthusiasm, and missionary zeal.

The challenge for the Korean American Catholic is to channel that zeal into a "beyond-Korean" vision that calls for Catholic unity. Inclusion not exclusion, universal one-community not monocultural enclaves and their attendant "ghetto-mentality" are the new keys to understanding the church. Jesus as a marginalized Jew urges a new perspective. The preoccupation of socio-economic domination is to be abandoned so as to adhere to the way of the Kingdom of God, where the first will be last and the last will be first. "The ills of today's church are fundamentally due to the seduction of a centralist inclination which does not perceive the actual presence of Jesus Christ at the margin."[6]

Korean American Catholics need to be on the front lines, promoting a solidarity and integral Christian humanism.[7] Instead of incomplete human formation, a wholesome, holistic human development is to be nurtured. Christian salvation is for all people and the whole person. Beyond individual wellbeing, a sense of responsibility in the spirit of solidarity is to be formed. In the public square, Korean American Catholics need to exercise "faithful citizenship" based on the Catholic social teaching. Pastoral plans and theological endeavors need to be more contextual, ecumenical, intercultural, relational, and dialogical so as to be Catholic.

Conclusion

Catholics as well as the whole world are sensing a radical new beginning through the graced leadership of Pope Francis. Through his ministry of mercy, Pope Francis presents us a radical call to envision a church faithful to Jesus' teaching and mission by reaching

---

6. Lee, *Marginality*, 122.

7. Pontifical Council for Justice and Peace, *Compendium*, 19.

out to the edges, the existential, social, and cultural peripheries. Jesus went to the outcast, the poor, prisoners and the sick, for those who were grieving and alone. Francis urges us to be "the poor church," "a church for the poor." Jesus was himself an outcast, rebuked by his racial brothers, condemned by the society he lived in, betrayed by his friends. And despite this, He showed us the way.

The early church, formed by the coming of the Holy Spirit on Pentecost, reveals the *radically transformed self-understanding* of the early Christians and hints at *a new human community and a new humanity*. This is not just an idyllic and ideal utopia but a reality realized and ever to be realized. The risen Christ sends the Holy Spirit from the Father and brings forth our communion with the Divine Persons and with one another.

By definition, a spiritual person is a relating and relational person. The church is the community of spiritually reborn people on that journey. The divinely initiated movement to engage us into a loving union with God and with one another is the *raison d'être* of the Church. The church's mission is to expand the concentric circles of communion in time and space. The Holy Spirit ever keeps us on our toes in the sacred tension of the already and the not yet, that is the very essence of an ongoing Pentecost.

Bibliography

Lee, Paul D. *Pneumatological Ecclesiology in the Roman Catholic-Pentecostal Dialogue: A Catholic Reading of the Third Quinquennium (1985–1989)*. Rome: Pontificiam Universitatem Studiorum Thomae, 1994.

Lee, Jung Young. *Marginality: The Key to Multicultural Theology*. Minneapolis: Fortress, 1995.

McDonnell, Kilian. *The Other Hand of God: The Holy Spirit as the Universal Touch and Goal*. Collegeville, MN: Liturgical, 2003.

Min, Pyong Gap. "Literature Review with a Focus on Major Themes." In *Religions in Asian America: Building Faith Communities*, edited by Pyong Gap Min and Jung Ha Kim, 15–36. Lanham, MD: Rowman & Littlefield, 2002.

Pontifical Council for Justice and Peace. *Compendium of the Social Doctrine of the Church*. Vatican: Libreria Editrice Vaticana, 2004.

Stelzer, Mark. "A New Ecclesial Reality and a New Way of Doing Theology: Heralding a New Pentecost." In *Many Faces, One Church: Cultural Diversity and the American Catholic Experience*, 13–26. Lanham, MD: Rowman & Littlefield, 2005.

Taylor, John V. *The Go-Between God: The Holy Spirit and Christian Mission*. London: SCM, 1972.

3

Korean American Catholics in the Changing American Religious Landscape

A Statistical Portrait

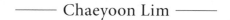

Chaeyoon Lim

DESPITE THE RECENT BOOM in sociological research on religion[1] and the growing interest in the religious life of new immigrant groups,[2] our knowledge of the religious life of Korean Americans is limited. To be sure, there have been excellent sociological studies of Korean American churches and the role of religion in Korean American communities, often focusing on Christian religions.[3] However, many of these studies rely on the case study method and ethnographic research, which are helpful in offering in-depth understanding of Korean American churches and religious

1. Smilde and May, "The Emerging Strong Program."

2. Yang and Ebaugh "Transformations in New Immigrant Religions"; Haddad et al., *Religion and Immigration*; Cadge and Ecklund, "Imigration and Religion"; Eklund and Park, "Religious Diversity and Community Volunteerism."

3. Kwon et al., *Korean Americans and Their Religions*; Min and Kim, *Religions in Asian America*; Chong, "What It Means to Be Christian"; Ecklund, *Korean American Evangelicals*.

experiences of Korean Americans but limited in providing a systematic bird's-eye view of religious life in the broader Korean American community.[4]

This limitation is largely attributable to the lack of high-quality quantitative data on the religious life of Korean Americans and Asian Americans in general. The US Census and other government surveys, such as the Current Population Survey and the American Community Survey, are the major data sources for social scientists who study demographic trends in the United States. Unfortunately, none of these data contain information about religion. As a result, most quantitative social science studies on religion in the United States rely on survey data, which sample a small number of Americans (typically a few thousand) to study values, attitudes, and behaviors of the US population. National surveys, including the General Social Survey (GSS) and surveys by Gallup and the Pew Research Center, have been useful sources for studying the religious experiences of Americans. Because these surveys aim to draw a "representative" sample of the US population, however, they typically interview only a handful of Asian Americans, let alone Korean Americans. The latest GSS in 2014, for instance, sampled twenty-two Chinese Americans and seven Japanese Americans. The number of Korean Americans was too low to constitute a separate category, and thus, they were merged with other Asian descendants in the "other Asians" category, which had eighteen respondents in total. Because of the small sample sizes in the GSS and other national surveys, it is impossible to use these surveys to study the religious experiences of Korean Americans in any systematic way or compare their experiences with other Asian Americans or with the general US population.

A small number of high-quality survey data that focus on Asian Americans have become available in recent years. In particular, the Pew Research Center's 2012 Asian American Survey (henceforth, the Pew survey) offers a unique opportunity to study the religious life of Korean Americans. First, the Pew survey interviewed a large number of Asian American adults eighteen years of

4. Cadge and Ecklund, "Immigration and Religion."

age or older (N = 3,511). The survey sample was designed to be representative of the Asian American population. More importantly for this chapter, the survey was also designed to represent the largest Asian subgroups, including Koreans.[5] To my knowledge, this is one of the very few surveys that have a nationally representative sample of Korean Americans. The survey included five hundred and four Korean Americans, 70 percent of whom are US citizens. About three quarters of Korean Americans in the survey are first generation, who came to the United States as adults. Only 11 percent are second-generation Korean Americans, who were born in the United States. In addition to having a large representative sample of Korean Americans, the Pew survey includes a number of questions about the respondents' religious experiences, including their religious background, current affiliation, and various measures of religious belief and practice. In short, the Pew survey probably provides the best data available to date for systematically studying the religious experiences of Asian Americans, especially Korean Americans.

In addition to the Pew survey, the 2008 National Asian American Survey data is utilized.[6] In this survey, which was conducted by a group of political scientists, more than five thousand Asian Americans and Pacific Islanders, including six hundred fourteen Koreans, were interviewed. Although the focus of the survey was the political and civic participation of Asian Americans, the survey contained several questions about religion, some of which were not in the Pew survey. In particular, I use these data to see how many Korean American Christians converted to Christianity as opposed to growing up as Christians and whether they converted before or after they arrived in the United States.

Using these data sets, this chapter aims to provide a systematic overview of the religious life of Korean Americans. To put the religious life of Korean Americans in perspective, I compare their religious life with that of other Asian American groups, as well as

5. See Pew Research Center, "Asian Americans: A Mosaic of Faiths," for more details of the survey.

6. Ramakrishnan et al., *National Asian American Survey, 2008.*

with that of the general US population and the Korean population in South Korea. I also examine how Korean Americans' religious beliefs and practices vary by age and generation (i.e., first vs. second generations). Although examining changes using cross-sectional data such as the Pew survey, which provides only a snapshot at a single point in time, is problematic, the comparison across age groups and generations offers hints about future challenges awaiting Korean American religious organizations.

Before we turn to Korean Americans' religious experiences, however, I will take a brief detour and sketch some of the major changes in the American religious landscape in recent years. Although Korean American communities tend to be concentrated in a few metropolitan areas and often in certain neighborhoods, the communities are not insulated from the rest of American society. This also is the case for Korean American religious institutions and the religious experiences of Korean Americans. To properly understand what is happening in the religious life of Korean Americans, therefore, it is crucial to situate them within the broader context of American religion. Much of what I discuss in the next section has been reported in more detail in numerous articles and books.[7] In this chapter I focus on some of the major trends in recent decades that provide the most relevant contexts for our discussion of the religious life of Korean Americans and particularly of Korean American Catholics.

The Changing Religious Landscape in the United States

Although America in the twenty-first century is still an unusually religious country, scholars recently began to observe that major changes have been taking place in American religions, some of which pose serious challenges to the conventional wisdom of American exceptionalism and raise the question of whether America is truly immune to the force of secularization. One trend that

7. Putnam and Campbell, *American Grace*; Chaves, *American Religion*; Voas and Chaves, "Is the United States a Counterexample?"

has drawn much scholarly and public attention is what is called "the rise of nones": the fast increase in the number of Americans who claim in national surveys that they have no religious affiliation or preference.[8] In Figure 1, I display the trend in the percentage of American adults (eighteen years or older) who say they have no religious preference (i.e., "nones") between 1972 and 2014. The figure is based on data collected by the General Social Survey, one of the most commonly used national survey data in social science, which has tracked American public opinions on a wide array of issues since 1972.

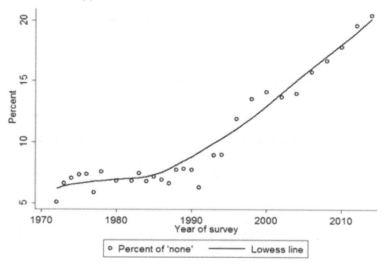

Figure 1. Percentage of "nones" in the General Social Survey 1972–2014
Note: Each circle represents the percentage of the GSS respondents who say they have no religious preference in each year. The solid line summarizes the trend over time (year of survey) using the Locally Weighted Scatterplot Smoothing (LOWESS) method.

Beginning in late 1980s or early 1990s, the percentage of "nones" has grown rapidly and continuously, and as a result, more than

8. Hout and Fischer, "Why More Americans Have No Religious Preference"; Hout and Fischer, "Explaining Why More Americans Have No Religious Preference"; Lim, Putnam, and MacGregor, "Secular and Liminal."

20 percent of Americans reported no religious affiliation in 2014, compared to 8 percent in 1990. A similar trend can be observed in many other national surveys in the United States, although the surveys differ in the exact inflection point and the precise size of the "none" population, partly due to the different procedures used to measure religious affiliation.[9] The most recent national survey conducted by the Pew Research Center (2015), in which more than 35,000 American adults were interviewed, puts the number of "nones" at 23 percent, even higher than the latest GSS estimate, suggesting no sign of a slowdown.

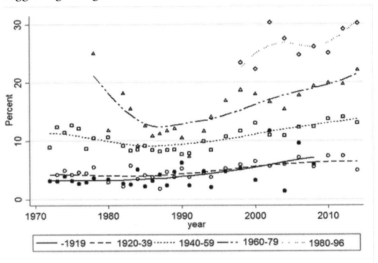

Figure 2. Percentage of "nones" by birth cohort
in the General Social Survey 1972–2014
Note: Each symbol represents the percentage of the GSS respondents who say they have no religious preference in each birth cohort. The lines summarize the trend over time (year of survey) for each cohort using the LOWESS method.

As several scholars have pointed out,[10] the rise of "nones" is largely driven by what sociologists call the "cohort effect": That is,

9. Lim et al., "Secular and Liminal."
10. Hout and Fischer, "Explaining Why More Americans Have No Religious

less religious younger cohorts replace more religious older cohorts, and as a result, society as a whole becomes less and less religious over time. Again using the GSS, Figure 2 shows the percentage of "nones" in each birth cohort (using an interval of about 20 years to define a cohort) by the survey year.[11] It is evident in Figure 2 that there has been a large increase in the percent of "nones" from cohort to cohort. Only about 5 percent of the people born before 1940 identified as "none" in 1970s, and even in the most recent surveys, the figure is no higher than 8 percent. In contrast, the percentage of "nones" in the youngest cohort of Americans in the GSS is close to 30 percent in the most recent survey in 2014. This is significantly higher even compared to the percentage of "nones" among older cohorts when they were still in their youth back in 1970s. Although there appears to be some increase within each birth cohort over time,[12] the data shown Figure 2 suggest that the cohort replacement has been and remains the main driver of the growth of the number of people with no religious affiliation in the United States.

Preference"; Voas and Chaves, "Is the United States a Counterexample?"

11. Similar to many other figures in this chapter, similar graphs have been produced by other scholars using the same data, including Putnam and Campbell, *American Grace*, and, more recently, Voas and Chaves, "Is the United States a Counterexample?"

12. This increase within each cohort is likely to be due to the large window (20 years) I used to define a cohort. Within each cohort, younger people are more likely to be "nones" and their percentage among the GSS respondents tends to increase over time.

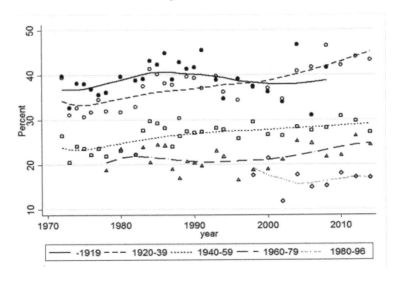

**Figure 3. Percentage of weekly churchgoers
in the General Social Survey 1972–2014**
Note: Each symbol represents the percentage of the GSS respondents who
say they attend religious services once a week or more often for each birth
cohort. The lines summarize the trend over time (year of survey) for each
cohort using the LOWESS method.

Although the decline in religious affiliation has received the
most attention, a similar, if subtler, change can be found in other
measures of religiosity. For example, Figure 3 shows the trend in
the percentage of Americans in each birth cohort who reported
that they attend religious services at least once a week. Again, we
observe a similar decline from cohort to cohort in weekly church
attendance. Compared to the oldest GSS cohort, 35 to 40 percent
of whom attended religious services at least once a week, only
about 15 percent of the youngest GSS cohort reported the same
level of attendance. Although weekly attendance seems to have ris-
en a little bit as the oldest cohort aged, it seems to remain stable in
the other birth cohorts, indicating that the overall level of church
attendance may not change much throughout one's life course.

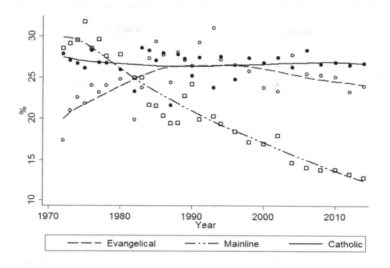

Figure 4. Trends in identification with three major Christian traditions in the General Social Survey 1972–2014
Note: Each symbol represents the percentage of the GSS respondents who identify with the given religious tradition. The lines summarize the trend over time (year of survey) using the LOWESS method.

The decline in religious affiliation and other measures of religiosity, however, has not affected all religions equally. In Figure 4, I present the trend in the percentage of Americans who identify with each of the three major Christian traditions in the US: Mainline Protestant (e.g., Presbyterian, Lutheran), Evangelical or Conservative Protestant (e.g., Southern Baptist), and Roman Catholic.[13] Figure 4 reveals that Mainline Protestants have experienced the largest decline, whereas Evangelical Protestants and Catholics have held their ground relatively well. This optimistic picture for Catholics, however, is somewhat misleading. Unlike Mainline Protestants, who tend to stop identifying with the tradition or

13. I follow a classification scheme commonly used by American sociologists of religion to group denominations into these three categories. See Steensland et al., "The Measure of American Religion," for details of the scheme.

denomination when their religiosity wanes, Catholics in America tend to hang on to their identity as Catholic, even when they no longer actively participate in religious life. Figure 5, which shows the trends in the percentage of regular churchgoers in the three traditions, illustrates this point. In this figure, I used monthly attendance (i.e., attending church at least once a month) instead of weekly attendance as the threshold to get a more conservative estimate of the decline in religious participation. Using weekly attendance yielded a similar pattern.

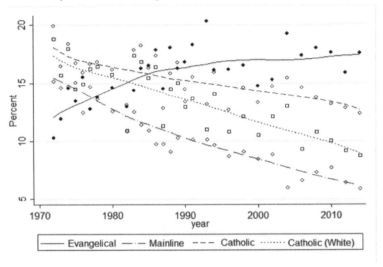

Figure 5. Trends in churchgoing members of three Christian traditions in the General Social Survey 1972–2014
Note: Each symbol represents the percentage of the respondents who identify with each religious tradition and attend religious services at least once of month out of all GSS respondents in the year. The lines summarize the trend over time (year of survey) for each religious tradition using the LOWESS method.

When we focus on the number of regular churchgoing members, the share of Catholics among American adults has declined significantly. This is particularly the case if we focus on regular churchgoing white Catholics. In other words, the seemingly stable trend for Catholics in Figure 4 obscures two important changes in American Catholicism. First, the number of churchgoing Catholics has declined significantly in the past few decades, although the number of people who identify as Catholic has remained stable. Second, the decline in identification and attendance among white Americans has been partly replenished by an inflow of Catholic immigrants, especially from Latin America.

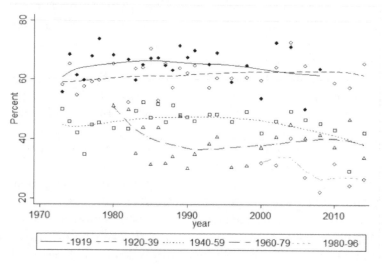

Figure 6. Trend in regular church attendance (at least once a month) among different cohorts of Catholics in the General Social Survey 1972–2014
Note: Each symbol represents the percentage of the Catholic GSS respondents in each birth cohort who attend religious services at least once a month or more often. The lines summarize the trend over time (year of survey) using the LOWESS method.

Finally, Figure 6 zooms in further on Catholics and looks at the percentage of regular churchgoers who attend religious services at least once a month, in each birth cohort among Catholics over time. The decline in attendance due to cohort replacement is evident in this figure. Compared to the cohorts born before 1940, more than 60 percent of whom attended church at least once a month or more often pretty much throughout their lives, less than 30 percent of the youngest cohort of Catholics in the GSS attended religious services once a month or more frequently. There are some changes within each cohort, which may be attributable to life course changes (e.g., returning to church after marriage or childbirth) or period effects, but such changes are small, and the level of attendance seems quite stable within each cohort of Catholics, implying that people may not change their habits of church attendance formed in youth significantly over their life course. This is troubling news for the Catholic church (and other major religious denominations in the US), given that the low level of attendance among younger cohorts of Americans may not change much as they age.

In summary, the religious landscape in America is going through significant changes, as a fast-growing number of people distance themselves from organized religions. This trend has not affected all religious traditions equally, and Catholics appear to have fared better than Mainline Protestants in terms of affiliation. However, the trend in religious affiliation obscures important changes in American Catholicism, including declining participation among younger people and the increasing presence of a non-white immigrant population. Thus, there is growing and indisputable evidence that Americans are gradually becoming less religious, no matter how their religiosity is defined and measured, and that this change is largely driven by cohort replacement, which is similar to what has happened in many other Western countries.[14]

Religious Life of Korean Americans

With these recent trends in American religion in the background, I now turn to the religious experiences of Korean Americans. I start by looking at the religious affiliation of Korean Americans and other Asian American subgroups in the Pew survey. Table 1 presents the distribution of religious affiliations in each Asian American subgroup. For comparison, the table also shows the distribution in the US population (based on the 2014 GSS) and the

14. Voas and Chaves, "Is the United States a Counterexample?"

Korean population in South Korea (using the data from the Pew Research Center's The Future of World Religions, 2015).

Table 1. Religious affiliation of the six largest Asian American groups in the Pew survey (%)

	Evangelical	Mainline	Catholic	Buddhism	Hinduism	None	Others	Total
Korean	40.4	20.9	10.2	5.7	0.0	22.6	0.2	100.0
Chinese	13.6	9.5	8.6	14.8	0.0	52.5	1.0	100.0
Filipino	15.1	9.2	66.4	0.5	0.1	8.5	0.1	100.0
Indian	11.8	3.6	5.2	0.9	57.0	11.3	10.3	100.0
Japanese	14.7	20.1	4.5	25.5	0.0	33.3	1.9	100.0
Vietnamese	2.6	3.6	30.3	43.4	0.0	19.9	0.2	100.0
All other Asians	12.2	9.8	9.8	27.9	9.3	27.7	3.5	100.0
Total	15.2	10.0	19.6	14.9	10.6	27.2	2.6	100.0
US Population[*]	24.0	12.9	26.7	1.1	0.6	21.8	13.0	100.0
Koreans in Korea[**]	17.9[***]		11.0	22.9	.	46.4	1.8	100.0

[*] The US population numbers are based on the 2014 General Social Survey
[**] The Korean numbers are based on the 2015 Pew Research Center's *The Future of World Religions* report.
[***] This is the percentage of Koreans who identify with any Protestant denomination.

A few things stand out in Table 1. First, Korean Americans are one of the largest Christian subgroups among Asian Americans. The only subgroup with a larger proportion of Christians is Filipinos, two thirds of whom are Catholic. Unlike among Filipinos, Protestants, especially Evangelical Protestants, are the largest religious group among Koreans, accounting for a little more than 40 percent of all Korean Americans, followed by Mainline

Protestants (20.9 percent) and Catholics (10.2 percent). The large number of Protestants among Korean Americans is remarkable given that less than 20 percent of Koreans in South Korea identify as Protestant. I will return to this issue shortly. Second, about 23 percent of Korean Americans report no religious affiliation, a figure not much different from the percentage of the general US population. As a result, "religious nones" are the second largest group among Korean Americans after Evangelical Protestants. Later, I break this group down further by age and generation to see whether the number of "nones" is also on the rise among young Korean Americans.

Table 2. Conversion experiences of Korean American Christians in the 2008 National Asian American Survey (%)*

Current religion	Have always been Christian	Converted before arriving in the US	Converted in the US	Total
Protestant	69.8	11.6	18.6	100.0
Catholic	70.6	12.6	16.8	100.0

*Only among the Korean Americans who were not born in the United States.

Why is the proportion of Protestants so much higher among Korean Americans than among Koreans in South Korea? There are two possible explanations. The first is selective migration: that is, Protestants in Korea may have a significantly higher probability of migrating to the United States than non-Protestant Koreans do. Another possibility is that a large number of Koreans convert to Protestantism when they arrive in the United States. To explore these possibilities, I turn to the 2008 National Asian American Survey, which asked all Christian respondents whether they had converted to Christianity, and if they had, whether they did it before or after they moved to the United States. Table 2 shows that among Koreans who were not born in the United States, about 70 percent of Christians (including Catholics) were raised as

Christians. This number does not vary between Protestants and Catholics. About 10 percent of the Korean American Christians born outside the United States converted before they arrived in the United States, meaning that in total eight out of ten Korean American Christians (either Protestant or Catholic) were already Christians when they arrived in the United States. In short, the unusually high proportion of Protestants among Korean Americans appears to be largely driven by the selective migration of Christians from Korea, although conversion after migration to the United States also contributed to some extent.

Table 3. Religiosity of the six largest Asian American groups in the Pew survey (%)

	Attending service		Importance of religion		Pray	
	Never	Weekly+	Not at all	Very	Never	Daily+
Korean	11.4	51.6	9.1	51.2	18.3	49.0
Chinese	32.0	17.7	23.7	20.9	36.4	19.1
Filipino	5.1	56.1	6.3	62.3	5.1	61.3
Indian	5.2	27.9	7.6	40.7	8.5	51.3
Japanese	23.2	16.9	17.9	28.2	27.2	30.4
Vietnamese	10.7	32.2	9.6	38.8	16.0	42.3
Other Asians	12.4	31.2	9.1	48.1	16.8	39.4
US population	26.2	24.7	7.0	56.0	7.0	58.0
Koreans in Korea	23.9	43.7	15.9	19.1	19.0	40.5

In Table 3, I return to the comparison of religiosity among major Asian American groups in the Pew survey. In this table, I use three indicators of religiosity: frequency of religious service attendance, frequency of prayer, and self-reported importance of religion in life. Regarding participation in organized religions, Table 3 suggests that Korean Americans are one of the most religious subgroups, not just among Asian Americans but also in the general US population. More than half of Korean Americans report that they attend religious services at least once a week or more often. This more than doubles the percentage of weekly churchgoers among the US population. Only Filipinos surpass Korean Americans in church attendance. Korean Americans are also highly religious, on average, in the other indicators of religiosity, but do not stand out as much as they do in religious service attendance. About half of Korean Americans report that religion is *very* important in their lives and pray daily, which is higher than the numbers for most Asian American groups other than Filipinos, but a little lower than the numbers in the general US population. In other words, Korean Americans, on average, are highly religious as a group, and they are particularly active in their participation in congregational life.

Table 4. Religiosity of major religious groups among Korean Americans in the Pew survey (%)

	Attending service		Importance of religion		Pray	
	Never	Weekly+	Not at all	Very	Never	Daily +
Evangelical	0.8	78.4	0.6	78.4	2.6	79.0
Mainline	8.3	55.8	0.4	42.7	2.8	43.1
Catholic	2.1	58.8	0.0	69.2	4.2	69.2
Buddhist	8.2	40.9	0.0	32.7	12.7	32.7
None	36.9	0.4	38.2	7.9	66.9	46.1

Table 4 further breaks down these indicators of religiosity among the major religious groups. Korean Americans in all three Christian groups are highly religious, but Evangelical Protestants stand out. Almost eight out of ten Korean Americans who identify with an Evangelical Protestant denomination attend religious services at least once a week. In fact, half of Korean American Evangelicals report that they attend religious services more than once a week. A similar number also pray daily and consider religion very important. Korean American Catholics are also highly observant.

The percentage of weekly churchgoers among Korean American Catholics is close to 60 percent, and more than two thirds of weekly churchgoing Catholics attend services more than once a week, not quite as high as among Evangelicals but much higher than the average weekly attendance among American Catholics in general, which was 24 percent in 2014. Among Korean Americans, Catholics also pray significantly more frequently and are more likely to consider their religion very important in life compared to Mainline Protestants.

In summary, Table 4 demonstrates that Korean Americans are, on average, remarkably religious, and it is the case for all major Christian traditions, although there are significant variations across the traditions. Compared to other Americans or Asian Americans, Korean Americans are particularly active in being involved with their congregations. Many reported that they attend services more than once a week. Even in Buddhism, which is traditionally not structured around a congregational model, 41 percent of the affiliates attend services at least once a week. In comparison, only one of ten Buddhists in the United States reported weekly attendance according to the recent GSS. The high level of engagement in congregations implies that religion serves as an important social organization in Korean American communities, through which people participate in community and social life.

Finally, one may be surprised to find that only 37 percent of the Korean American "nones" never attend a religious service, and quite a few express religion as an important aspect in life. In fact, about 46 percent say that they pray daily. This, however, is a well-documented phenomenon in the sociology of religion. Americans who claim no religious affiliation are not necessarily atheists or agnostics. In fact, the majority believe that God exists, and some even attend religious services regularly. A study by Lim and his colleagues (2010) showed that when "none" Americans were asked about their religious affiliation again a year later, about a third claimed an affiliation, meaning that many of them still have some, if weak, connections to organized religions. The fact that many Korean Americans with no affiliation pray regularly and think religion is important may imply that they have spiritual needs that are not adequately met by existing religious institutions.

My analyses of the Pew survey thus far show that Korean Americans are an unusually religious group, even when compared to the most religious racial or ethnic groups in the United States. Although Evangelical Protestants are the most religiously observant among Korean Americans, other groups, including Catholics, are also highly religious. Unfortunately, the Pew survey offers only a snapshot of Korean Americans' religiosity at one point in time, making it difficult to know how their religiosity has changed over time and in which direction it may be heading. With no data that track Korean Americans' religious life over time, the only option is to look at the patterns across different age groups among Korean Americans for insights into the changes in Korean Americans' religiosity. Table 5 looks at religious affiliations among Korean Americans by age group.

Table 5. Religious affiliation in different age groups among Korean Americans in the Pew survey (%)

	Evangelical	Mainline	Catholic	Buddhism	No religion	Others
18–34	33.1	14.0	6.5	5.1	40.6	0.6
35–49	50.5	18.4	9.1	2.6	19.5	0.0
50–64	37.0	27.7	12.5	9.4	13.5	0.0
65 or older	38.6	24.3	13.2	6.3	17.2	0.4
Total	40.4	20.9	10.3	5.7	22.6	0.2

There are some notable patterns in religious affiliation across age groups among Korean Americans. First, the percentage of religious "nones" is significantly higher among younger Korean Americans, especially among those under thirty-five years old. In fact, the percentage of "nones" among Korean Americans under thirty-five (40.6 percent) is significantly higher even in comparison to the same age group in the US population (29 percent). Second, the percentage of mainline Protestants and Catholics declines significantly from older to younger age groups. Among the youngest age group, less than 7 percent identify as Catholic, as opposed to 13 percent among Korean Americans sixty-five years of age or older. In comparison, the decline among Evangelicals seems less pronounced, with the highest percentage in the thirty-five to forty-nine age group. As a result, Catholics are, on average, older than Evangelical Protestants or any other groups among Korean Americans. Korean American Catholics' mean age is 56.5, compared to 53.7 among Evangelicals and 47.5 among the "nones." These patterns across age groups imply that increasing "nones" among Korean Americans may have come largely at the expense of Catholics and mainline Protestants. Table 6 offers some evidence for this possibility.

Table 6. Religious switching among Korean Americans in the Pew survey (%)

Religion as kid	Current Religion				
	Evangelical	Mainline	Catholic	Buddhist	No religion
Protestant	53.8	25.0	1.7	0.8	18.8
Catholic	14.6	11.3	47.0	1.1	26.1
Buddhist	21.4	23.3	9.6	32.0	13.8
No religion	37.5	16.8	7.0	2.6	35.0
Total	40.4	20.9	10.2	5.7	22.6

Table 6 compares the religion in which Korean Americans grew up, with their current religious affiliation at the time of the survey. Of Korean Americans who grew up in a Protestant family, for example, almost 80 percent stayed in the tradition, either as Evangelicals (53.8 percent) or mainline Protestants (25 percent); whereas a little less than 19 percent switched to no religious affiliation. In contrast, only 47 percent of those who were Catholic growing up remained in the same tradition. More than a quarter switched to "none," and another quarter now identify as Protestant. Moreover, Catholicism is not a popular destination for people who grew up with different religious backgrounds. Among people who grew up with no religion, only 7 percent switched to Catholicism, whereas more than half became Protestant. Even among Korean Americans who were Buddhists as children, more identified as Protestants now than as Buddhists. In short, among Korean Americans, Catholicism seems to be the "biggest loser" in this "switching game" of religion, failing to retain children with a Catholic background and not succeeding in attracting people from different backgrounds.

Table 7. Religiosity of different age groups
among Korean Americans in the Pew survey (%)

	Attending service		Importance of religion		Pray	
	Never	Weekly +	Not at all	Very	Never	Daily+
18–34	14.1	40.1	13.9	41.0	29.8	21.2
35–49	12.2	48.7	7.6	49.2	17.8	52.5
50–64	11.0	48.1	9.4	49.8	12.8	56.1
65 or older	8.2	69.5	6.1	65.0	12.8	65.9
Total	11.4	51.6	9.1	51.2	18.4	49.0

Returning to the patterns of religiosity among different age groups of Korean Americans, the low level of religiosity among young Korean Americans is visible in all three indicators (Table 7). Weekly church attendance declines from almost 70 percent among the oldest group to 40 percent among the youngest, self-reported importance of religion from 65 to 41 percent, and daily prayer from 66 to barely over 21 percent. Even though young Korean Americans are significantly more likely to report no affiliation than average young Americans do, they overall still look quite observant compared to the same age group in the US population. This is largely because young Korean Americans who report a religious affiliation are unusually observant. Although not shown in Table 7, two thirds of Korean Americans under thirty-five with a religious affiliation attend religious services weekly or more often; the equivalent figure among all Americans in the same age group is

23 percent. In other words, young Korean Americans who identify with organized religions are still highly religious, but the percentage of Korean Americans with a religious affiliation is significantly smaller than that among young Americans in general.

Table 8. Religious affiliation and religiosity of the first and second generation of Korean Americans in the Pew survey (%)

	First generation	Second generation
Religious affiliation		
Evangelical	41.6	38.6
Mainline	20.5	21.6
Catholic	12.2	7.0
None	17.1	31.1
Attend religious service at least weekly	61.8	35.9
Religion is very important in life	57.8	41.2
Pray daily or more often	57.8	36.1

Finally, Table 8 shows a breakdown of religious affiliation and religiosity between the first and second generations of Korean Americans. Because of the small sample size, I include people who came to the United States before they turned eighteen years old (the 1.5 generation) in the second generation. Consistent with the patterns by age groups presented above, second-generation Korean Americans are more likely to identify with no religion (31 percent) and are significantly less observant in any measure of religiosity than the first generation. However, the decline in affiliation is substantial only for Catholics. In fact, the percentage of Evangelicals or mainline Protestants is quite consistent between the generations. Together with the patterns we observed earlier, this finding suggests that Catholics may have been more deeply influenced by the intergenerational decline in religiosity than the other Christian traditions among Korean Americans.

Conclusion

Overall, my analysis of the Pew survey paints a coherent but complex picture of changing religious experiences of Korean Americans. Although Korean Americans are one of the most religious groups in the United States and exceptionally active in their participation in congregational life, young Korean Americans are even more likely to be disaffiliated from organized religions than average young Americans are. At the same time, however, young Korean Americans who remain religiously affiliated are substantially more observant than average young Americans who do. In a sense, young Korean Americans seem to be religiously polarized, with highly observant affiliates on the one hand and a large and growing group of non-affiliated who are secular in their beliefs and practices on the other. This generational change, however, has not affected religious groups evenly. Catholicism has experienced the largest decline between the generations in affiliation and other measures of religiosity; whereas Evangelical Protestantism seems to have held its ground fairly well, partly by retaining children within the tradition but also by attracting people who grew up in different religious backgrounds. In contrast, Catholicism has lost more than half of the people who grew up in the tradition to "nones" or to Protestant denominations, while only attracting a handful of converts from other traditions. As a consequence, Korean American Catholics are aging faster than other religious groups. Needless to say, this is a concerning demographic trend for Korean American Catholic communities and the wider US church.

These trends suggest that the Korean American community is not insulated from the rest of American society, and whatever forces that have been transforming the American religious landscape in recent years are also casting their influence on Korean Americans. In fact, there are good reasons to suspect that these changes may be accelerating instead of slowing down, especially among this ethnic faith group. Korean Americans, on average, are highly educated, socially and politically liberal, and concentrated in urban population centers on the coasts. All these factors are strong predictors of non-affiliation and secular attitudes and behaviors, meaning that these social and demographic forces are likely to make the situation more challenging for Korean American churches.

The challenge seems to be particularly tall for Korean American Catholic churches. The percentage of "nones" is rising the fastest among those who grew up as Catholics. Unlike Korean American Protestant churches that recruit actively from people with no or different religious backgrounds, Catholic churches attract few new adherents. Explaining why Catholic churches are struggling more than Protestant churches in the Korean American community is beyond the scope of this chapter. However, this significant variation between religious traditions, with some traditions more successful in meeting the challenges than others, suggests that the intergenerational decline in religiosity may not be inevitable.

It is also notable that young Korean Americans who remain affiliated with religion are still unusually observant, especially compared to other young Americans whose religious beliefs and participation are sagging even among the affiliates. In addition, the Korean American community has a constant inflow of new immigrants from Korea. It is unclear whether the selective migration of Christian Koreans we observed earlier is still the case, but recall that at least 20 percent of Korean American Christians converted to Christianity after they arrived in the United States. As many scholars have pointed out, Korean American churches have served as a central social institution that helps newcomers settle in and provide them with social connections and a sense of belonging.[15] This role of the Korean American church as a "social hub" is probably responsible for the unusually high level of religiosity among Korean Americans, especially their participation in congregation. In short, several factors are in favor of Korean American churches, although it is uncertain whether these countervailing forces are sufficient to offset the larger trends in American religion and the demographic challenges facing the Korean American religious community.

15. E.g., Min, "Korean Immigrant Churches"; Ley, "Immigrant Church as an Urban Service Hub."

Bibliography

Cadge, Wendy, and Elaine Howard Ecklund. "Immigration and Religion." *Annual Review of Sociology* 33 (2007) 359–79.

Chaves, Mark. *American Religion: Contemporary Trends*. Princeton, NJ: Princeton University Press, 2011.

Chong, Kelly H. "What It Means to Be Christian: The Role of Religion in the Construction of Ethnic Identity and Boundary among Second-Generation Korean Americans." *Sociology of Religion* 59, no. 3 (1998) 259–86.

De Graaf, Nan Dirk. "Secularization: Theoretical Controversies Generating Empirical Research." *The Handbook of Rational Choice Social Research* (2013) 322–54.

Ecklund, Elaine Howard, and Jerry Z. Park. "Religious Diversity and Community Volunteerism among Asian Americans." *Journal for the Scientific Study of Religion* 46, no. 2 (2007) 233–44.

Ecklund, Elaine Howard. *Korean American Evangelicals: New Models for Civic Life*. Oxford: Oxford University Press, 2006.

Gorski, Philip S., and Ates Altinordu. "After Secularization?" *Annual Review of Sociology* 34 (2008) 55–85.

Haddad, Yvonne Yazbeck, et al., eds. *Religion and Immigration: Christian, Jewish, and Muslim Experiences in the United States*. Walnut Creek, CA: AltaMira, 2003.

Hout, Michael, and Claude S. Fischer. "Explaining Why More Americans Have No Religious Preference: Political Backlash and Generational Succession, 1987–2012." *Sociological Science* 1 (2014) 423–47.

Hout, Michael, and Claude S. Fischer. "Why More Americans Have No Religious Preference: Politics and Generations." *American Sociological Review* 67, no. 2 (2002) 165–90.

Kim, Kwang Chung, et al. "Korean American Religion in International Perspective." In *Korean Americans and Their Religions: Pilgrims and Missionaries from a Different Shore*, edited by Ho-Youn Kwon, Kwang Chung Kim, and R. Stephen Warner, 3–24. University Park, PA: Pennsylvania State University Press, 2001.

Kwon, Ho-Youn, et al. *Korean Americans and Their Religions: Pilgrims and Missionaries from a Different Shore*. University Park, PA: Pennsylvania State University Press, 2001.

Ley, David. "The Immigrant Church as an Urban Service Hub." *Urban Studies* 45, no. 10 (2008) 2057–74.

Lim, Chaeyoon, et al., "Secular and Liminal: Discovering Heterogeneity among Religious Nones." *Journal for the Scientific Study of Religion* 49, no. 4 (2010) 596–618.

Min, Pyong Gap. "The Structure and Social Functions of Korean Immigrant Churches in the United States." *International Migration Review* 26, no. 4 (1992) 1370–94.

Min, Pyong Gap, and Jung Ha Kim, eds. *Religions in Asian America: Building Faith Communities*. Walnut Creek, CA: AltaMira, 2001.

Pew Research Center. "Asian Americans: A Mosaic of Faiths." July 19, 2012. http://www.pewforum.org/2012/07/19/asian-americans-a-mosaic-of-faiths-overview/.

Pew Research Center. "The Future of World Religions: Population Growth Projections, 2010–2050." April 2, 2015. http://www.pewforum.org/files/2015/03/PF_15.04.02_ProjectionsFullReport.pdf.

Pew Research Center. "U.S. Public Becoming Less Religious." November 3, 2015. http://www.pewforum.org/2015/11/03/u-s-public-becoming-less-religious/.

Putnam, Robert, and David E. Campbell. *American Grace: How Religion Divides and Unites Us*. New York: Simon & Schuster, 2012.

Ramakrishnan, Karthick, et al. *National Asian American Survey, 2008*. Ann Arbor, MI: Inter-university Consortium for Political and Social Research, 2011. doi: 10.3886/ICPSR31481.v2

Smilde, David, and Matthew May. "The Emerging Strong Program in the Sociology of Religion." *Social Science Research Council Working Paper*, February, 2010.

Steensland, Brian, et al. "The Measure of American Religion: Toward Improving the State of the Art." *Social Forces* 79, no. 1 (2000) 291–318.

Voas David, and Mark Chaves. "Is the United States a Counterexample to the Secularization Thesis?" *American Journal of Sociology* 121, no. 5 (2016) 1517–56.

Yang, Fenggang, and Helen Rose Ebaugh. "Transformations in New Immigrant Religions and their Global Implications." *American Sociological Review* (2001) 269–88.

4

The Family of God

Resurrection and Eternal Life in Korean Catholicism and the Western Tradition

 James K. Lee

As a Korean American scholar of early Christianity, I am challenged to consider how my research relates to my identity as a Korean American Catholic. How might the study of the early Church contribute to a deeper understanding of Korean American Catholicism? What might early Christian studies have to offer the Church today? I have discovered that there is much to offer, not least in terms of preserving particularity in the midst of diversity. That is, we find in early Christianity a way to affirm particular identities while seeking unity. Living in a pluralistic society, I encounter the tendency to seek unity at the cost of diversity, resulting in uniformity. However, in the early Church, unity comes not at the expense of diversity, but as its logical consequence.[1]

The principle of unity in diversity applies not only in terms of the global growth of the Church, but also with regard to certain

---

1. Burns, "Establishing Unity in Diversity," 381–99.

fundamental theological commitments of Christianity.[2] For instance, the doctrine of the bodily resurrection of the dead provides an illustration of the preservation of particularity and diversity, for it means nothing less than a return to particular bodies. Therefore, this study explores Catholic views of bodily resurrection and eternal life in the history of the Western tradition, and in Korean Catholicism as it developed in the eighteenth and nineteenth centuries. It seeks to identify what is held in common, and what remains distinctive to these traditions. In doing so, it considers the significance of Catholic teaching on eternal life for contemporary Korean American Catholic identity. In my experience as a Korean American, there is a growing temptation to leave behind difference in the pursuit of uniformity. In the history of Christianity, we discover a way to embrace distinction in the midst of a diversity that will be preserved for eternity.

I begin by examining the thought of perhaps the most influential Western theologian in the history of Christianity, Augustine of Hippo (ca. 354–430 CE).[3] Augustine provides the foundation for Western Catholic reflection upon eternal life, yet much of the richness of his thought, especially on the resurrection of the body, has been neglected. I offer a renewed look at Augustine's teaching on eternal life by exploring works such as *De doctrina Christiana*, *De catechizandis rudibus*, and *De civitate Dei*, with a focus on bodily resurrection.

Next, I turn to Korean Catholic views of heaven and eternal life among the Korean martyrs, particularly Augustine Jeong Yakjong (1761–1801 CE), who was among those beatified by Pope Francis in August 2014. Augustine Jeong compiled the first Korean catechism, a work that was highly influential in the growth of Catholicism in Korea, and which provides insight into distinctively Korean views of eternal life, including an emphasis on heaven as

---

2. On the diversity and growth of early Christianity, see Meeks and Wilken, *Jews and Christians*; Hengel, *History of Earliest Christianity*; Hurtado, *At the Origins*; Wilken, *First Thousand Years*.

3. Levering, *Theology of Augustine*, xi–xii.

a place of family reunion.[4] I argue that this emphasis upon familial reunion represents an authentic development of the Catholic tradition.

Finally, I will consider how to appropriate such traditions in a contemporary context, and how such an appropriation bears meaning for Korean American Catholic identity. On the one hand, Korean American Catholics share in the received tradition of the universal (*catholica*) Church, while on the other hand, they have the opportunity to carry forward the distinctive tradition of the Korean martyrs, who offer a witness of hope in the joy and glory of eternal life.

Augustine of Hippo (354–430 CE)

Augustine's thought on eternal life has been the most influential in the history of the Western tradition. Brian Daley observes that Augustine's teaching is "in most of its details, thoroughly traditional, based on the accumulated theological resources of the Eastern Church since Origen and the Western Church since Tertullian and Hippolytus, as well as on the practices and the cherished hopes of African Christians in his own day."[5] Augustine's theology was forged in the context of the North African tradition of martyrdom. He often celebrated the Eucharistic liturgy and preached in commemoration of the martyrs on feast days, and his works give witness to North African knowledge of the martyrdom of Perpetua and Felicitas, among others.[6]

For Augustine, the Church is primarily a communal, social body, the one body of Christ, with many members. The lives of the martyrs serve as a pledge of the glory to be revealed for the whole Church as members of the body of Christ. The unique sacrifices of the martyrs testify to the unity of the Church in the midst of

---

4. Rausch, "Dying for Heaven," 213–34; cf. Kim and Kim, *A History of Korean Christianity*, 30–31

5. Daley, *Hope of the Early Church*, 131.

6. Cf. *De anima et eius origine* 4.18.26–27; *Enarrationes in Psalmos* (*Enarrat. Ps.*) 47.13; *Sermones* (*Serm.*) 280–82, 394; *Serm.* Dolbeau 159A.

diverse forms of persecution and suffering.[7] Further, their acts of sacrifice stand in opposition to the pagan sacrifices of the Roman Empire, and thereby offer a kind of resistance to the imperial regime.[8] Thus, the witness of the martyrs impacted Augustine's theology not only in terms of his writings on the unity and nature of the Church against sectarian groups such as the Donatists, but also in his developing argument against the pagans in works such as *De civitate Dei*.

Eternal Life

For Augustine, eternal life consists of the vision of God (*visio Dei*),[9] yet as he makes clear in *De doctrina Christiana*, this vision is a *shared* vision. The vision of God is a communal sharing in the light and life of the Trinity, for "the light of truth reveals God as Trinity (*Trinitas*), who provides for all the things he has made as author and maker of the universe."[10] The final end of human beings is the enjoyment of God, for "enjoyment consists in clinging to something lovingly for its own sake,"[11] and "a thing is to be loved for its own sake" if it "constitutes the life of bliss" (*in eo constituitur beata vita*).[12] God alone constitutes the life of bliss, yet as Augustine argues, the enjoyment of God is not a solitary act. Instead, the "supreme reward is that we should enjoy [God] and that all of us who enjoy him should also enjoy one another in him."[13] Thus, the

7. On Augustine's understanding of martyrdom, see Straw, "Martyrdom," 538–42.

8. Cavadini, "Ideology and Solidarity," 93–110.

9. *De civitate Dei* (*Civ.*) 22.29. *De civitate Dei* was completed over the course of 413–427 CE.

10. *De doctrina Christiana* (*Doctr. chr.*) 1.10.10; Corpus Christianorum Series Latina (CCSL) 32, p. 12. Translation follows Hill, *Teaching Christianity*, 110. *De doctrina Christiana* was begun in 396 CE and completed ca. 426/427 CE.

11. *Doctr. chr.* 1.4.4 (*Teaching Christianity*, 107).

12. *Doctr. chr.* 1.22.20 (*Teaching Christianity*, 114).

13. *Doctr. chr.* 1.32.35 (*Teaching Christianity*, 122); cf. 1.22.21–23.22, 27.28–29.30, 33.37, 39.43.

final end of humanity is a *shared* enjoyment of God rather than a kind of isolated vision.

The shared enjoyment of God is made possible by the one mediator between God and humanity, Jesus Christ, who is the way to the Father.[14] Christ unites the distinctive members of his body in charity, for "while his body consists of many parts, having different functions, he binds it tightly together with the knot of unity and love, as its proper kind of health."[15] As the one mediator, Jesus leads the members of his body to the Father and the Holy Spirit. Just as the Holy Spirit is the love between the Father and the Son, so too the Spirit is the love shared between the members of the Church,[16] and the Spirit "binds" and "glues together" the members so that they may remain in the "supreme and unchangeable good."[17] For Augustine, the Church's members remain unique, yet together they form a fellowship united in the love of God (*in societate dilectionis Dei*).[18] During this time, the Church remains on pilgrimage on earth until all of her members reach the heavenly "homeland" (*patria*).[19]

At the end of earthly life, the souls of the dead are immediately judged, and either come to share in the vision of God, or receive the just punishment due to the wicked.[20] However, the rewards and punishments experienced by the dead are only a hint of their final destinies, which will be realized at the general resurrection of the body.[21] This is the eschaton or "end time," when Christ will come in glory, and all the dead will be raised either to everlasting joy or to eternal damnation. Far from a fearful expectation, the

---

14. *Doctr. chr.* 1.34.38.

15. *Doctr. chr.* 1.16.15 (*Teaching Christianity*, 113).

16. *De Trinitate* (*Trin.*) 5.11.12; 15.17.29.

17. *Doctr. chr.* 1.34.38; cf. *Trin.* 6.5.7; 7.3.6.

18. *Doctr. chr.* 1.29.30 (*Teaching Christianity*, 119).

19. *Doctr. chr.* 1.4.4; cf. 1.9.9.

20. *Civ.* 13.8; *De praedestinatione sanctorum* (*Praed.*) 12.24; Daley, *Hope of the Early Church*, 137.

21. *Serm.* 328.6.5; *Epistuale* (*Ep.*) 159.4; *In Evangelium Johannis tractatus* (*Tract. Ev. Jo.*) 49.10; Daley, *Hope of the Early Church*, 137.

resurrection of the dead is the hope of Christians, for "if the dead do not rise again, there is no hope of a future life for us; but if the dead do rise again, there will indeed be a future life."[22]

For Augustine, bodily resurrection means the restoration of the same bodies in which we labored on earth.[23] As he declares in *De catechizandis rudibus*,[24] "at the time God wishes, he will restore all things without any delay or difficulty . . . thus human beings will come to render an account of their deeds in the same bodies in which they performed them, and in these bodies they will receive what they deserve."[25] God is the creator of both souls and bodies, and God will be the restorer of both.[26] The visible flesh will rise again,[27] yet following Paul in 1 Cor. 15, Augustine maintains that the risen body will be a "spiritual body," one that is no longer corruptible, and no longer wars against the spirit, but is perfectly subject to the human will.[28] There will be a complete integration between body and soul, such that souls will be perfectly content in physical bodies.[29]

Augustine goes on to speculate about the nature of the resurrected body in order to deal with objections raised by opponents of Christianity.[30] The resurrection will be a reassembling of all the particles of matter that originally belonged to the individual, yet reshaped according to harmony and proportion.[31] Parts of the body that have been discarded, such as nails and hair, will not nec-

22. *Serm.* 361.2 (translation follows Hill, *Sermons*, 225); Daley, *Hope of the Early Church*, 141–42.

23. *Civ.* 13.19; cf. *Serm.* 256.2; Daley, *Hope of the Early Church*, 143.

24. Ca. 400 CE.

25. *De catechizandis rudibus.* 25.46; Canning, *Instructing Beginners in Faith*, 156.

26. *Serm.* 277.3; Daley, *Hope of the Early Church*, 143.

27. *De fide et symbolo* (*Fid. symb.*) 10.23; Daley, *Hope of the Early Church*, 143.

28. *Civ.* 13.20; 22.21; *Serm.* 242.8.11; Daley, *Hope of the Early Church*, 143.

29. *Civ.* 22.26; Daley, *Hope of the Early Church*, 144.

30. Daley, *Hope of the Early Church*, 144.

31. *Civ.* 22.19; *Enchiridion ad Laurentium* (*Enchir.*) 23.87; Daley, *Hope of the Early Church*, 144.

essarily be reclaimed in the same form, nor will there be disfigurements of size and shape.[32] Further, those who have died as infants or small children will receive additional matter in order to rise in the size they would have reached had they lived to maturity, which Augustine speculates as the age of thirty-three, after the pattern of Christ.[33]

Moreover, resurrected bodies will be in a transfigured state, as evident in *De civitate Dei* 22, in which Augustine suggests that the bodies of the martyrs will bear the wounds which "they suffered for Christ's name," yet "in their case these will not be marks of deformity but marks of honor."[34] Just as Christ bears the marks of his passion and death in his resurrected body in glorified form, so too the members of Christ's body, i.e. the Church, will bear the marks of their suffering in a glorified way. The sufferings of each member are unique, born from the Church's pilgrimage in history, and the Church's journey leads to the resurrection of the "whole Christ" (*totus Christus*) as a transfigured, glorified body.[35]

While Augustine's reflections on the nature of the resurrected human body remain speculative, two considerations in particular stand out. First, Augustine claims that all of the organs of the body will be restored in ideal form, even though many will not be used.[36] This includes the sexual organs, and the sexual identity of men and women will be retained as a sign of the unity and solidarity for which human beings were created.[37] The fact that human beings retain their sex reveals how humanity is uniquely social and communal by nature, not in an external fashion, such as the way

32. *Civ.* 22.19; *Enchir.* 23.89; Daley, *Hope of the Early Church*, 144.

33. *Civ.* 22.14; *Enchir.* 23.85; *Serm.* 242.2; Daley, *Hope of the Early Church*, 144.

34. *Civ.* 22.19 (translation follows Babcock, *City of God,* 530).

35. In *Civ.* 22.21, the resurrected body is a "spiritual body, clothed in incorruptibility and immortality," for it is no longer "carnal" and subject to the struggle of the "flesh." This resurrected body is a mystery, yet it is a true body "subdued to the spirit," and the philosophers such as Porphyry deny such a resurrection (*Civ.* 22.25–28).

36. *Serm.* 243.4, 7; Daley, *Hope of the Early Church*, 144.

37. *Civ.* 22.17; Daley, *Hope of the Early Church*, 144.

birds form flocks.[38] Instead, human beings are created in order to become a member of a fellowship (*societas*), and to enter into unity with others, as evidenced in the complementarity of the sexual organs of men and women. The Church is united as one body, the body of Christ, just as Adam and Eve are united as one flesh (Gen. 2:24), prefiguring the mystery of Christ and the Church (Eph. 5:30).[39]

Second, Augustine considers whether after the resurrection, the blessed will see God "face to face" with their transformed bodies.[40] For Augustine, the direct contemplative vision of God is the heart of beatitude, yet this is a kind of "spiritual vision" whereby one clings to God as one's final end and enjoyment. Augustine concludes that a corporeal vision of God is unlikely, yet in the final book of *De civitate Dei*, he suggests that just as our eyes now "see" life in other bodies by looking at them, so too the eyes of the spiritual body will be able to "see" God in their own way, as present in all of the transformed universe, and as the source of life for all creatures.[41] Thus, the blessed will see all of creation as evidence of God's glory, as further reason to offer praise.

For Augustine, heaven does not consist of a kind of passive contemplation; rather, it will consist of an activity all its own, namely, the activity of praise.[42] The life of the saints is a life of praise without ceasing.[43] Every part of the resurrected body will play its part in praising God.[44] In this resurrected form, the Church will be perfected "in its angelic fullness," and will form one eternal community united in praise.[45] Heaven is essentially social and ecclesial,

---

38. *Civ.* 12.28.

39. *Civ.* 14.13; 15.1, 20, 22, 26; 18.1, 51; 19.17.

40. *Civ.* 22.29; Daley, *Hope of the Early Church*, 145.

41. *Civ.* 22.29; Daley, *Hope of the Early Church*, 145–46.

42. *Enarrat. Ps.* 85.24; Daley, *Hope of the Early Church*, 146.

43. *Serm.* 362.30.31; Daley *Hope of the Early Church*, 146.

44. *Civ.* 22.30.

45. *De consensu evangelistarum* 2.75.145; *Serm.* 303.2; *Ep.* 148.2.8; 187.5.16; *Enchir.* 9.29; Daley, *Hope of the Early Church*, 146–47.

and it consists of a perfectly ordered and harmonious *societas* of those who enjoy God, and who enjoy one another in God.[46]

These two aspects of the resurrected body point to the communal nature of the eternal life given by Christ. On several occasions, Augustine speaks of the Church as the "family" (*familia*) of God[47] or the family of Christ,[48] "gathered from all nations" in "incorruptible flesh."[49] Just as Noah and his family was marked by water and the wood of the ark, so too the family of Christ, the Church, is marked by baptism.[50] Augustine invokes the family as a way to imagine the society of the saints, yet his primary way of conceiving of the Church is as a communal body, the one body of Christ, united in charity.

At the eschaton, there will be a final restoration of bodies, and the martyrs will bear the wounds of their suffering, not in deformity but in glory, just as Christ bears the wounds of his passion and suffering in his glorified body. This principle applies to all who come to share in Christ's life and glory; that is, all of the members of Christ's body will bear the marks of their suffering in this life as marks of love in their resurrected bodies. These wounds will be transfigured and transformed, so as to reveal the depths of love signified by bodily suffering. The resurrection of the body will be a visible revelation of the depth, height, and breadth of Christ's victory over death.

For Augustine, the Church's celebration of the Eucharist anticipates the final eschatological kingdom by uniting the heavenly city with the city of God on earthly pilgrimage as the one body of Christ. At the Eucharistic altar, the Church offers the one sacrifice of Christ, the high priest, "under the form of a servant" (Phil. 2:6), in union with the sacrifices of the members of the body.[51]

---

46. *Civ.* 19.13; Daley *Hope of the Early Church*, 147.

47. Cf. *Contra secundam Juliani responsionem imperfectum opus* (*C. Jul. op. imp.*) 6.40.9; *Civ.* 1.29.

48. *Contra Faustum Manichaeum* (*Faust.*) 12.14; *Civ.* 1.35.

49. *C. Jul. op. Imp.* 6.40.9.

50. *Faust.* 12.14.

51. *Civ.* 10.6, 20.

This is the "supreme," "total" sacrifice of the "whole Christ" (*totus Christus*), that leads the members to cling to God as their final end and final happiness.[52] Citing Romans 12, Augustine asserts that the members of the body are conformed to Christ the head, and this is the offering by which the Church shows that "she herself is offered" as the sacrifice pleasing and acceptable to God.[53] In this Eucharistic offering, the one sacrifice of Christ, the supreme work of mercy, infuses all of the sacrifices of the Church, making them true sacrifices and "works of mercy" (*opera misericordiae*) that unite the one city of God in anticipation of the eschaton,[54] when all of the works of mercy offered as sacrifices out of the two-fold love of God and neighbor will be revealed in the fullness of glory and in a permanent fashion, as marks and signs of charity forever borne on the bodies of the saints. Until then, the Eucharist is the source and summit of the Church's life during her earthly journey, in anticipation of the final eschatological communion.

Augustine Jeong Yak-jong (1761–1801)

The Korean martyr Jeong Yak-jong, whose namesake is Augustine, compiled and edited the first catechism in Korean entitled the *Chugyo yoji* (Essentials of Catholicism).[55] This work was likely written in the late 1790s, and it relies heavily upon various books in Classical Chinese, yet it shows little or no accommodation to Confucian thought.[56] The catechism was circulated widely and re-

52. *Civ.* 10.20.

53. *Civ.* 10.6.

54. Ibid.

55. Rausch, "Dying for Heaven," 216; Kim and Kim, *History of Korean Christianity*, 30–31.

56. The catechism "was an adaptation of a Chinese catechism with the same name by Luigi Buglio, an Italian Jesuit (probably utilizing some material from the Riccian approach of Yi Byeok and the reasoning of Jeong Yak-jong's brother Dasan . . . *Jugyo Yoji* shows little or no accommodation to Confucian thought. It follows a Scholastic form of catechism beginning with logical arguments for God's existence and the doctrine of the Trinity. Compared to Buglio's work, it gives greater emphasis to criticism of Buddhism and folk religion and

mained in print through the twentieth century, and thus it played a significant role in shaping Korean Catholic views of eternal life.

In its narrative of the afterlife, the catechism offers a traditional, orthodox account of death, judgment, and the Second Coming and General Judgment, based upon the death and resurrection of Jesus.[57] Jesus' suffering merited not only his own resurrection, but also the promise of a new and glorious life. Yet before the full revelation of this new life, God will bring judgment to the world, preceded by great calamities. Following the judgment, the good will be sent to heaven, while the evil will be sent to hell. Heavenly joy consists of the vision of God, for the more one sees God, the more pleasure increases.[58] By contrast, hell consists of eternal sufferings.

According to the catechism, heaven is a place of immeasurable joys where the blessed gather together with Jesus as "companions and siblings" of "countless angels and saints."[59] Heaven is depicted as a place of family reunion, and this means not only reunion with the members of one's family from this world, but also union with all of the members of the family of God, i.e., the saints and angels.[60] For Catholics in Korea, the "church valorized the relationship between fellow believers, terming it [kyo hyeong], 'brother in faith,' and taught . . . that such a relationship is more intimate than that of biological siblings."[61] This distanced Korean Catholics from the Confucian orientation toward shared ancestry that demanded claims of affection and worship.[62] Thus, Korean Catholicism emphasized familial reunion, while at the same time

---

to the doctrines of judgment and heaven and hell" (Kim and Kim, *History of Korean Christianity*, 30). Cf. Noh, *History of Korean Catholic Church*, 80–129.

57. Rausch, "Dying for Heaven," 216–18.

58. Ibid.

59. Ibid., 217.

60. Ibid., 215, 225, 229.

61. Kwang, "Human Relations," 32; Cho points out that the *Sŏnggyŏong chikhae* cites the views of the fourth-century church father John Chrysostom.

62. Ibid.; cf. Choi, "Ancestor Worship," 35–43; Baker, "Catholicism in a Confucian World," 199–230.

relativizing sibling relationships in order to forge bonds with the entire body of Christ, such that all of the saints and angels may be considered part of the one family of God.

Franklin Rausch rightly observes that the vision of afterlife depicted in the *Chugyo yoji* "stands squarely within Catholic orthodoxy," and "does not appear to be that different from other Catholic catechisms published elsewhere."[63] Thus we find in Korean Catholicism a clear continuity with the Western Catholic tradition on matters of death and eternal life, yet there is a pronounced emphasis upon familial reunion. This is evident, for instance, in the letters of Korean martyrs such as Luthgarde Yi Sun-i (1782–1802), and her brother, Paul Yi Gyeong-eon (d. ca. 1827). For these siblings, the hope of heaven includes family reunion, and this enabled them to persevere in the midst of persecution. It also provided comfort for those who had to give up familial duties such as Paul, who asked his older brother to look after his family while promising that should he be taken to heaven, he would help his family to get there.[64] This promise extended not only to his family, but also to other members of the Myongdohoe (Society for Illuminating the Way).[65]

The distinctive contribution of Korean Catholicism to the Church's teaching on eternal life is an emphasis upon the transformation of communal relations in familial terms. To enter heaven is to become a "sibling of the saints." As we have seen, this idea is not foreign to the thought of Western Fathers such as Augustine of Hippo, yet it is more pronounced in the Korean tradition, and there is an added focus on reunion with one's earthly family in heaven. Although there is no explicit mention of familial reunion in the works of Augustine of Hippo, this idea is in line with his

---

63. Rausch, "Dying for Heaven," 218.

64. Ibid., 223–29.

65. The Myongdohoe was an organization established by the Chinese priest Father James Zhou Wen-mo dedicated to encouraging Catholics to practice the faith zealously, and to do missionary work; Rausch, "Dying for Heaven," 216; Kim and Kim, *History of Christianity*, 34–35.

notion of the Church as the one family of God and the one body of Christ, united in charity.

Further, for both Augustine of Hippo and Augustine Jeong, the distinction of the members enhances rather than diminishes union. This is the case above all in the example of the martyrs, who will bear the glorified wounds of their suffering in their resurrected bodies. Each member is unique and irreplaceable, taking a particular place in the body of Christ. Following the Korean tradition, each saint will be reunited with his or her family, and these distinctive familial relations will not be forgotten, but instead will be retained, while at the same time the saint will be joined to the entire communion of saints and angels, united as the one family of God.

A Theological Appropriation

How might one appropriate the insights of Western and Eastern Catholic views of eternal life, as represented by Augustine of Hippo and Augustine Jeong Yak-jong respectively? This requires an exercise of the theological imagination, with an eye toward the final judgment and the general resurrection of the body. According to Augustine of Hippo, all the saints will rise again, bearing in their bodies the glorified wounds of love, in conformation to Christ. This is not only a restoration of the physical body, but also a transformation and transfiguration of creation, and a perfect and harmonious ordering of all things in praise of God. The saints and angels will enjoy the vision of God as a communal body, a vision that means a participation in the Triune life of love, and a clinging to that good which is our final end and rest.

In the midst of this union in charity remains the diversity of creation, and in particular the diversity of bodies among the saints, who bear the glorified wounds of their particular experiences and sacrifices. It follows from an Augustinian eschatology that the unique attributes of the physical body will be retained, according to harmony and proportion. Thus, the diversity of creation will not be eliminated at the resurrection, but instead will be restored and transformed, in order to reveal the glory of the Creator. The martyrs, such as Paul Yun Ji-chung and companions, will rise again and bear the wounds of love in their bodies, as witnesses in their particular historical contexts. These bodies share a story of love and offer a narrative of the triumph of Christ's sacrifice in every era. In this eschatological state, the memory of the martyrs' suffering will not be lost, but rather will be on display to lead all to the praise of God.

Following the Korean Catholic emphasis upon family reunion, it is entirely consistent to hope that the distinctive familial bonds formed during this earthly life will not be lost for eternity. Instead, these bonds will be remembered and restored, yet reconfigured such that all come to share in the one family of God. The union in charity of the one body of Christ does not destroy diversity, but rather is predicated upon such diversity so as to create new bonds of union.

Korean American Catholicism

This theological exercise of the imagination bears meaning for Korean American Catholics, who carry forward the traditions of both East and West in a pluralistic context. In this setting, Korean American Catholics have the opportunity to provide a witness that affirms diversity and particularity, yet with the aim of union in charity that can only be achieved by the merits of Christ, the mediator. It is Christ who conquers death and gives life, and who incorporates the distinctive members of the Church into his body, while preserving their distinctive identities (cf. 1 Cor 12). The Church's hope in eternal life and the resurrection of the body must be renewed in every generation, and Korean American Catholics have the opportunity to provide a witness of hope as bearers of history and tradition. What might this look like? I suggest three essential characteristics of this witness.

First, the Church's hope in the eternal life given by Christ does not undermine or eliminate the significance of earthly life. This is not to be confused with a "pie in the sky" theology that, in effect, cheapens the Church's journey in history. On the contrary, the promise of heavenly glory and the resurrection of the body elevates the meaning of history and adds an eternal dimension, for all sacrifices and acts of love offered in this life will be retained and glorified, in some way, at the resurrection of the body. What we do in this life will be preserved for eternity, for the praise and glory of God.[66] Our hope, therefore, does not devalue this life, but rather gives it greater significance due to our final destiny. This is an important theological consideration for the witness offered by Korean American Catholics in a society that seeks to undermine Christianity as an "other-worldly" religion.[67]

Second, given the emphasis upon familial reunion in the afterlife in Korean Catholicism, Korean American Catholics would do well to seek to retain familial bonds and connections, despite the fragmentary nature of contemporary society as a result of immigration and dispersion. The preservation of family ties is a witness for the whole Church and for global Christianity, which continues to grow in a secular, pluralistic world. The growth of Catholicism does not require a rejection of culture and ethnic identity, but rather provides a way to integrate and incorporate particular identities, precisely insofar as they are taken up into the mystery of Christ's unifying love. Distinctive familial and ancestral bonds are not destroyed, but rather are transformed and reconfigured within the mystical body of Christ, which consists of many members, bound together in the love of God and neighbor.

Third, though not all are called to physical martyrdom, the Church's members can offer small acts of love and sacrifice, offered in union with the Eucharistic sacrifice of Christ. At the Eucharistic altar, the sacrifice of the whole Christ, head and members, is offered, as one body and one family. The Eucharist is the memorial of Christ's sacrifice, and at the same time a pledge of "future glory,"[68] the glory of the risen Christ. From this liturgical celebra-

---

66. Levering, *Theology of Augustine*, 145: "The key point is that what we do in time carries forward into life after death."

67. Rausch, "Dying for Heaven," 229.

68. *Catechism of the Catholic Church* 1323.

tion, the members of the Church are sent out in order to proclaim the Good News, and to offer works of mercy. The hope of Christians, therefore, is a Eucharistic hope, yielding love of God and neighbor. Korean American Catholics must remember and carry forward the unique tradition of Augustine Jeong and the Korean martyrs, but also remain grounded in the Eucharistic identity of the Church, so as not to live in isolation from the communal body of Christ. Just as Korean American Catholicism honors the past, so it must look to the future, when Christ will come in the fullness of glory to bring into unity the one family of God.

Bibliography

Augustine. *Answer to Faustus.* The Works of Saint Augustine I/20. Translated by Roland Teske. New York: New City, 2007.

————. *The City of God.* The Works of Saint Augustine I/6 and I/7. Translated by William Babcock. New York: New City, 2012–2013.

————. *Contra Faustum Manicheum.* Corpus Scriptorum Ecclesiasticorum Latinorum 25.1. Vienna: Tempsky, 1891.

————. *Contra Iulianum opus imperfectum.* Corpus Scriptorum Ecclesiasticorum Latinorum 85.1–2. Vienna: Tempsky, 1974.

————. *De anima et eius origine.* Corpus Scriptorum Ecclesiasticorum Latinorum 60. Vienna: Tempsky, 1971.

————. *De catechizandis rudibus.* Corpus Christianorum Series Latina 46. Turnhout: Brepols, 1969.

————. *Instructing Beginners in Faith.* Translated by Raymond Canning. New York: New City, 2006.

————. *De civitate Dei.* Corpus Christianorum Series Latina 47–48. Turnhout: Brepols, 1955.

————. *De consensu Euangelistarum.* Corpus Scriptorum Ecclesiasticorum Latinorum 43. Vienna: Tempsky, 1904.

————. *De doctrina Christiana.* Corpus Scriptorum Ecclesiasticorum Latinorum 80. Vienna: Tempsky, 1963.

————. *De fide et symbolo.* Corpus Scriptorum Ecclesiasticorum Latinorum 41. Vienna: Tempsky, 1900.

————. *De praedestinatione sanctorum.* Patrologia Latina 44. Paris, 1841.

————. *De Trinitate.* Corpus Christianorum Series Latina 50/50A. Turnhout: Brepols, 1968.

————. *Enarrationes in Psalmos.* Corpus Christianorum Series Latina 38–40. Turnhout: Brepols, 1990.

————. *Enchiridion ad Laurentium de fide spe et caritate.* Corpus Christianorum Series Latina 46. Turnhout: Brepols, 1969.

————. *Enchiridion on Faith Hope and Charity.* Translated by Bruce Harbert. New York: New City, 1999.

————. *Epistulae.* Corpus Scriptorum Ecclesiasticorum Latinorum 34, 44, 57, 58, 88. Vienna: Tempsky, 1895–1981.

————. *Expositions of the Psalms.* The Works of Saint Augustine III/14–17. Translated by Maria Boulding. 4 vols. New York: New City, 2000–2002.

————. *Faith and Creed.* Translated by Edmund Hill. In *On Christian Belief.* The Works of Saint Augustine I/8. New York: New City, 2005.

————. *The Harmony of the Gospels.* Translated by S. D. F. Salmond. Nicene and Post-Nicene Fathers 6. Grand Rapids, MI: Eerdmans, 1994.

————. *Homilies on the Gospel of John (1–40).* Translated by Edmund Hill. The Works of Saint Augustine III/12. New York: New City, 2009.

————. *In Iohannis euangelium tractatus.* Corpus Christianorum Series Latina 36. Turnhout: Brepols, 1954.

————. *Letters.* Translated by Roland Teske. The Works of Saint Augustine II/1–3. New York: New City, 2001–2005.

————. *The Predestination of the Saints.* Translated by Roland Teske. In *Answer to the Pelagians IV.* The Works of Saint Augustine I/26. New York: New City, 2000.

————. *Sermones.* Corpus Christianorum Series Latina 41. Turnhout: Brepols, 1961.

————. *Sermons.* Translated by Edmund Hill. The Works of Saint Augustine III/1–11 (11 vols.). New York: New City, 1991–1997.

————. *Teaching Christianity.* Translated by Edmund Hill. The Works of Saint Augustine I/11. New York: New City, 1996.

————. *The Trinity.* The Works of Saint Augustine I/5. Translated by Edmund Hill. New York: New City, 1991.

Baker, Don. "Catholicism in a Confucian World." In *Culture and the State in Late Chosŏn Korea,* edited by JaHyun Kim Haboush and Martina Deuchler, 199–230. London: Harvard University Press, 1999.

Burns, J. Patout. "Establishing Unity in Diversity." *Perspectives in Religious Studies* 32, no. 4 (2005) 381–99.

Catholic Church. *Catechism of the Catholic Church.* 2nd ed. Washington, DC: USCCB, 2000.

Cavadini, John C. "Ideology and Solidarity in Augustine's *City of God.*" In *Augustine's City of God: A Critical Guide,* edited by James Wetzel, 93–110. New York: Cambridge University Press, 2012.

Choi, Ki-bok. "Ancestor Worship: From the Perspective of Confucianism and Catholicism." In *Ancestor Worship and Christianity in Korea,* edited by Jung-young Lee, 35–43. Lewiston, NY: Mellen, 1988.

Daley, Brian E. *The Hope of the Early Church: A Handbook of Patristic Ecclesiology.* Peabody, MA: Henrickson, 2003.

Dolbeau, F. Augustine d'Hippone: *Vingt-six sermons au peuple d'Afrique.* Paris: Études Augustiniennes, 1996.

Hengel, Martin. *Acts and the History of Earliest Christianity.* Translated by John Bowden. Philadelphia: Fortress, 1980.

Hurtado, Larry. *At the Origins of Christian Worship.* Grand Rapids, MI: Eerdmans, 2000.

Kim, Sebastian, and Kirsteen Kim. *A History of Korean Christianity.* Cambridge: Cambridge University Press, 2015.

Kwang, Cho. "Human Relations as Expressed in Vernacular Catholic Writings of the Late Chosŏn Dynasty." In *Christianity in Korea,* edited by Robert E. Buswell Jr. and Timothy S. Lee, 29–37. Honolulu: University of Hawaii Press, 2006.

Levering, Matthew. *The Theology of Augustine: An Introductory Guide to His Most Important Works.* Grand Rapids, MI: Baker Academic, 2013.

Meeks, Wayne, and Robert Louis Wilken. *Jews and Christians in Antioch in the First Four Centuries of the Common Era.* Missoula, MT: Scholars, 1978.

Noh, Yong-pil. *A History of Korean Catholic Church*. Seoul: Korean History, 2008.

Rausch, Franklin. "Dying for Heaven: Persecution, Martyrdom, and Family in the Early Korean Catholic Church." In *Death, Mourning, and the Afterlife in Korea: From Ancient to Contemporary Times*, edited by Charlotte Horlyck and Michael J. Pettid, 213–34. Honolulu: University of Hawaii Press, 2014.

Straw, Carole. "Martyrdom." In *Augustine Through the Ages: An Encyclopedia*, edited by Allan D. Fitzgerald et al., 538–42. Grand Rapids, MI: Eerdmans, 1999.

Wilken, Robert Louis. *The First Thousand Years: A Global History of Christianity*. New Haven, CT: Yale University Press, 2013.

5

Seasons of Belonging

St. Thomas Aquinas as a Guide for Korean American Catholics

 Andrew Kim

I AM A THIRD-GENERATION, biracial Korean American. Through my childhood, I learned to regard identity through a framework of binary-oppositionalism: I learned to think that embracing my American identity meant negating my Korean one. I took my Korean and American identity as contrary things that could not be joined in a harmonious whole. While in graduate school however, I was drawn to the thought of St. Thomas Aquinas and it is through his theory of the unification of the moral self that I learned a way out of this kind of thinking. Perhaps one of the most distinctive features of Thomistic thought is the refusal to rest content with lazy binaries of this kind. For example, different philosophical eras have emphasized either the material or spiritual nature of the human person. Aquinas taught that we are a composite of body and soul. Different theological eras have emphasized grace over against nature or nature over against grace, but Aquinas maintained that grace perfects nature. It is these two sets of apparent contraries—body and soul, grace and nature—upon which I shall focus my thoughts in the current section. After having done so, I shall reflect upon how these aspects of Thomistic theology help me work through my Korean American identity.

Aquinas understood the soul as "the first principle of life in those things which live."[1] He laments that the "philosophers of old" did not grasp this as they wrongly asserted that "only bodies were real things; and that what is not corporeal is nothing."[2] Aquinas thought this was a mistake. The human experience cannot be summed up in the activities of organs, neurons, and nerves. We are intellectual beings with the capacity to discern true from false and good from evil. We have a spiritual nature by which we seek to arrive at accurate knowledge of divine things. In our day, the material reduction of the human person has again become fashionable. Powerful forces are at work constantly telling us that we are nothing more than a collection of atoms that happen to interact in a certain way. Energy and matter in motion is all there is. Our deepest yearnings for God, truth, and goodness are put on the same level as a craving for a jelly donut. All is instinct. The human person is shaped by natural selection to have certain appetites and aversions. In such a framework, the spiritual life of man is dismissed as a fanciful illusion that one must simply outgrow. Such a view, then, teaches us that there is no comfort to be found outside of material things. The refusal to recognize the importance of the spiritual life turns man into a self-serving machine racing through a life of tragic wastage, trudging forward like fodder and trying not to collide with the other.

The opposite danger is to depreciate the bodily life of person by adopting a false spiritualism that lessens the physical world of which God is the author. Though we human beings cannot be reduced to our bodies, neither can we negate the reality of our bodies. In addition to being spiritual beings, we are physical beings. We are embodied. We have instincts and desires and needs. This, too, is an essential part of the human condition. At the heart

1. Aquinas, *Summa Theologiae*, Ia, q.75, a.1.
2. Ibid.

of Catholic teachings, we find the doctrine of the Incarnation. In the person of Jesus Christ God became man in a way that did not negate but elevated and completed our human nature. There were separatists in the early Church who taught that Jesus did not actually possess a physical body as they saw this as depreciating the divine, as pulling the divine down into the earthly. However, sound doctrine has always held that in the Incarnation the human is lifted up into a higher synthesis while retaining all that which is essentially and distinctively human. We are not, then, either body or soul; we are a composite of body and soul.

Another set of apparent contraries that Aquinas reconciles are grace and nature. Imagine a man sitting by a pond repeatedly tossing a small stone up into the air, catching it, and then tossing it up again. Aquinas explained that it is unnatural for the stone to ascend. All he meant was that stones do not naturally move upward in the air, nor can they move themselves upward by an internal principle. Therefore, the only way a stone can move upwards is through an external cause, like a man tossing it up into the air. The man has the power to apply force to the stone so as to make it behave in a way that is contrary to its stony nature. Now, there were some theologians who held that the Fall basically reduced man to the status of a stone with respect to performing good deeds. We had become so depraved by sin that we could no longer do any good deeds without God taking over our wills, as it were. However, Aquinas recognized that if the only way we did anything good was by God using us as instruments, like a carpenter uses an ax, then no action of ours could ever be blameworthy or praiseworthy.

There are two types of error that generally follow from discussions of grace and nature. The first is the one I have just finished describing that regards grace as basically negating and supplanting our nature such that the divine will supersedes and replaces our human freedom. The other view overemphasizes our human capacity to choose and do good things in a manner that leaves no room for grace to be operative in our lives. Aquinas overcame both errors by holding that grace perfects nature without negating it. Because God is a "very powerful moving cause," God is able to transform our natures and draw us to Himself without negating our freedom. We freely choose to participate in God's plan for our lives by accepting God's divine help. Even this acceptance of grace is made possible by grace. However, this is accomplished in a manner that does not diminish our own volition in choosing to accept help. If the Holy Spirit used our wills as the carpenter uses an ax, then "all human merit would disappear," since the only "actions that are meritorious are those that are in some sense up to us." However, this does not prevent the Holy Spirit from "moving the soul to a loving action . . . of its own accord rather than under compulsion."[3]

It is this coming together of seeming contraries into a harmonious whole that I was most attracted to in the thought of St. Thomas Aquinas. At the time, I did not stop and ponder why I found this attractive or whether it had something to do with the difficulties I faced that in some sense are distinctive of my experience as a Korean American. Reflecting upon it now, I am inclined to think that these difficulties are something immigrant populations (even third generation immigrants like me but probably more so for first and second generation immigrants) encounter. One extreme response is that of assimilation. This is the response I am more familiar with; it entails leaving behind one's cultural background in order to perceive oneself as fully American. The other extreme is to form a cultural enclave and resist assimilation into the wider culture in which one finds oneself. I think the preferable approach dwells somewhere in the middle. The Korean identity and cultural heritage is not a rival to American identity and heritage. Both are, after all, different variants of universal human experiences. Furthermore, all Americans that are not Native Americans (and really even they) descend from immigrants somewhere along the way.

Certain people with limited theological imaginations seem capable of only seeing destruction in the creation of something new. They could not comprehend the Jesus who was and is both

3. Aquinas, *De caritate,* a.1. See also Kim, "Have the Manicheans Returned?," 451–72.

fully God and fully man, because they saw only the humanness encroaching upon the divine or the divine supplanting the human. The mystical synthesis frustrated them and blinded them from God's providential and creative activity in the world. There are those who couldn't appreciate the composite of body and soul that is the human person, because they preferred man to be purely physical or purely spiritual. There are those that can only respect grace as a repudiation of nature or regard nature as authentic only when separated from divine activity. Finally, there are those who can only see in the coming together of different cultural and ethnic strands the negation of two different cultural identities instead of recognizing God's providential bringing together of dissimilar things in order to create something new. Failing to appreciate God's creative activity in the world is a failure to appreciate God's providence, and failing to appreciate God's providence leads to ignorance of God. And this ignorance is something that I, as a Korean American, appropriated into my own understanding at an early age. I think a lot of us do this. We learn it from a culture that does not know how to categorize us. In a sense, we are uniquely prone to it. In the fullness of the Catholic tradition we are invited to a new and richer self-understanding. The coming together into a harmonious whole of our Korean and American selves is not an impossibility but an opportunity. We are not accidents of time and chance or even the choices of our parents or our parents' parents. That we should be here with our unique points of view, eccentricities and experiences is part of God's design. God has a specific purpose for us, aspects of which I shall now consider.

As I stated earlier, the main reason why I felt compelled to negate my Korean heritage was because I wanted to feel like I fully belonged. I wanted the comfort of belonging. I noted also that this desire can be a dangerous one as, in the pursuit of belonging, we are often all too willing to compromise aspects of our authentic identities. The desire to belong can become an idol. However, this touches upon a theme that is not unique to Korean Americans. Catholics believe that God has created us for more than this world. We are ultimately called, in Aquinas's language, to belong to the "society of the blessed" or "heavenly Jerusalem."[4] We are citizens of this world, but also of a higher kingdom. This raises the issue of how we are to be in the world but not of the world.

I have argued previously that to embrace the teachings of the Catholic Church puts one at odds with much of secular society.[5] There arises, then, a mentality among many Catholics to turn away from much that is distinctive in our identity in order to please modern society. If our theology is too supernatural, we replace it with a more palatable "this-worldly" emphasis. If our morality is too absolute, we replace it with a divinely underwritten situation ethics. If our liturgy is too full of adoration, we turn it into a coming together for coffee, donuts, and gossip that happens to be preceded by a mass. In order to belong to this world and not feel in conflict with it we shed all that which is prophetic and otherworldly and turn the Church into a mere social club or political organization. This is similar to the assimilationist approach that I described earlier. Belonging to the world entails repudiating our Catholic identity. The opposite approach is to retreat from the world and form a little Catholic enclave or holy huddle disconnected from the ordinary lives of people, standing in many ways in condemnation over those people. This mentality regards the Church as a kind of holy island or fortress. Embracing one's Catholic identity entails repudiating the world.

The Korean American experience helps us appreciate the need to eschew both of the approaches I just finished describing.[6] Indeed, as Catholics we are called to recognize that the Church forms a part of "the whole human family."[7] It is not that we are either members of the Church or members of the human family. We are members of both and it is in this context and with this understanding that we are to work in partnership with others for the salvation of the individual and the renewal of society. Thus it is that our belonging in the blessed society informs our belonging

4. Aquinas, *De caritate*, a.2.

5. Kim, *Introduction to Catholic Ethics*.

6. See also Kim, "Aquinas and Hauerwas," 311–25.

7. Paul VI, *Gaudium et Spes*, no. 3

in the earthly society. That which is distinctive about our Catholic identity is not something to be suppressed or turned into a weapon of exclusion. Rather, it is something we must marshal in order to communicate with others "the saving resources which the Church has received from its founder under the promptings of the Holy Spirit."[8]

As Korean American Catholics we pass through different seasons of belonging. We feel in a powerful way societal forces that seek to conform us into a host of prepackaged identities that conceal the true self and our vocations as Catholics. I think that we experience this both as Korean Americans attempting to embrace the different cultural strands that went into making us but also as Catholics trying to live by a code that the world often finds unintelligible and unworthy. Thus, let us use our experience as Korean Americans to help remind the Church of her true identity and calling. The Church is called to instill the "family spirit" among the various and disparate groups that make up humanity.[9] When religion goes bad it becomes just another source of strife, conflict, and alienation, but true religion does just the opposite. True religion brings contrary things together into a harmonious whole. True religion reconciles the self to God and neighbor and brings inner peace through the strength of grace. It ends the long war.

In sum, growing up as a third generation, bi-racial Korean American created in me an intense desire to belong. I came to view in a negative light the aspects of my identity that made me different. As a result, I suppressed my Korean self in favor of my American self. One of the reasons that I was drawn to the theology of Thomas Aquinas, though I did not realize it at the time, had to do with the manner in which he was able to conceive of seemingly rival aspects of one's identity as forming a creative synthesis that reflected the wisdom and goodness of an all-powerful God. Our ultimate desire is to belong to the society of this God and it is only here where a lasting comfort can be found. It is only then that the desire to belong ceases to be an idol. It is the striving after of

8. Ibid.

9. Paul VI, *Gaudium et Spes,* no. 42.

this belonging that is to inform our belonging to the earthly city. As Korean Americans we must at some point decide to reconcile the contrary strands of identity within our very persons. We may view this as part of God's plan for our lives. If it is part of God's plan, then it is not without purpose. Let us, therefore, as Korean American Catholics, direct the fruits of our labors and introspection so as to shed additional light upon the Church's vocation to form the human race into a single family where our differences are not used to foster hatred and petty rivalries but rather embraced as evidence of God's ongoing presence and creative activity in the world that God has not abandoned but redeemed through Jesus Christ.

Bibliography

Aquinas, Thomas. *Summa Theologiae.* Translated by the Fathers of the English Dominican Province. New York: Benziger, 1948.

————. *Questions on Virtue: Quaestio disputata de virtutibus in communi, Quaestio disputata de virtutibus cardinalibus, de fraterni correctionis.* Edited by E. M. Atkins and Thomas Williams, translated by E. M. Atkins. Cambridge: Cambridge University Press, 2005.

————. *On Love and Charity: Readings from the Commentary on the Sentences of Peter Lombard.* Translated by Peter A. Kwasniewski. Washington, DC: Catholic University of America Press, 2008.

Kim, Andrew. *An Introduction to Catholic Ethics since Vatican II.* New York: Cambridge University Press, 2015.

————. "Have the Manicheans Returned? An Augustinian Alternative to Situationist Psychology." *Studies in Christian Ethics* 26, no. 4 (2013) 451–72.

————. "Aquinas and Hauerwas on the Religious and the Secular." *New Blackfriars* 96 (2015) 311–25.

Paul VI (pope). *Gaudium et spes.* December 7, 1965. http://www.vatican.va/archive/hist_councils/ii_vatican_council/documents/vat-ii_const_19651207_gaudium-et-spes_en.html.

6

Imagine! An Examination of Race and Gender in Korean American Catholicism

— Hoon Choi —

IN HIS *LETTER TO the Romans*, St. Paul instructs believers to *Rejoice in Hope* as a sign of improving relations and uniting Christians of different persuasions. St. Paul's conviction is that if we put our trust in God, we will truly rejoice knowing that our hopes for this unity inevitably will come true. A similar challenge exists for Korean American Catholics today with differing viewpoints of gender and sexuality. Korean American Catholics are bombarded with different teachings from multiple sources in this regard. Their views are formed by the general social norms and expectations of gender and sexuality prevalent in American society and by the ways in which they themselves are (negatively) perceived by that society. Their perspectives are also informed by the official Roman Catholic teachings and practices. Their own Korean heritage further complicates the issue because neo-Confucian patriarchal norms and cosmology are still operative within Korean American Catholic settings. The result of these multilayered messages from multiple sources is confusion.

I will address some of these sources that contribute to the confusion, suggest ways in which these multilayered identities can come together to form a new life-giving energy, and extract from this process of identity formation my proposition that this confusion can be transformed into an opportunity for grace. This conversion is possible if Korean American Catholics learn from and emulate the early Christians, Korean martyrs and, most importantly for this chapter, the Trinity. We realize that we are made in the image of a Triune God and a part of the Christian vocation is to emulate God. The multiple personae of the Trinity are not in competition but in a balanced movement, a harmonious dance, if you like, among them. Thus, Korean American Catholics can imitate and learn from God's dance.

How do we navigate through and harmonize our multiple personae? That is one of the tasks of our current project. For my part, I make this effort from the vantage point of gender and sexuality. If we paid attention to our gendered being, we would learn that these multiple embodied identities that make us stay intact are supposed to be celebrated, appreciated, and harmonized. In the end, by paying attention to their gendered selves, Korean American Catholics can discover the unifying grace and, indeed, the mystical "one body" that reveals God and God's self-communication in and through Korean American Catholic stories and experiences.

American Gender Expectations

There is no "pure" gender. From the earliest stages of our lives, we are molded by our parents. Often, parental decisions to have their child(ren) dress and play in certain ways are influenced by the surrounding culture, which has a great impact on what we learn, say, teach, and believe about gender. Certainly, one of the most influential sources is popular culture. In a fast-moving and globalized world of technology and gadgets, even the most passive and remote participant of society is influenced by popular culture with its commercials, sports, movies, music, games, reality TV shows, audition programs, magazines, etc. These constructs of American (for the purposes of this paper) popular culture often limit one from fully expressing oneself integrally and authentically. In a way, we are "boxed in" by these constructs.

Women are often presented as nurturing and domestic. Hence, instead of showing their capacity to succeed in both domestic and professional realms, women are regularly depicted dichotomously. If they are not "domestic," they are either "hypersexual," and therefore seen as sexual objects or dangerous femmes fatales, or "professionals" and therefore "denounced as a threat to the moral order of traditional mothering," allowing a singled life as the only other viable alternative for women professionals.[1] When women are trapped in this "Woman Box," anything outside the box is seen as deviant and irresponsible, leaving them only a dichotomized option of being "virtuous housewives or child(ren) and family-neglecting workaholics."[2] For men, there is an assumption of dominance, aggression that feeds into the stereotypes: "Men and boys do not cry, they are tough, and they are sexual and powerful."[3] Moreover, there is a certain acceptance in the American culture of crude, childish, loud, goofy, inept, and unintelligent men.[4] When men are trapped in the "Man Box" they are effectively "cut . . . off from certain traits such as creativity, kindness, and attentiveness."[5]

Furthermore, not all women and men are stuck in their boxes equally. White men continue to dominate in the majority of front page stories in America. This heteronormative typecast not only sets white men as entitled and "normal" but also reduces American imagination to a vision of white-male stereotypes.[6] One of the possible implications that stems from this sort of inculcation is that to be a white man is to be normal/beautiful. If he is not born white, he can at least attempt to resemble someone who is. Another pos-

---

1. Frechette, "Gender and Femininity," 127. Such socialization happens very early on in boys' lives, which comes with an expectation of social status.

2. Ibid., 128.

3. Tarrant, "Gender and Masculinity," 139.

4. Westerfelhaus, "Gender and Masculinity," 135–36.

5. Tarrant, "Gender and Masculinity," 139.

6. Ibid., 139–40.

sible implication, deduced from the first, is that if one is born a woman, at least she can be, or strive to look, Caucasian. Some may argue that such a norm is a phenomenon of the past. However, we discover a manifestation of this norm as recent as January 2015 in Hollywood. The nominations for the Academy Awards for acting went to 20 all-white actors and actresses in the year that witnessed, most notably and at the very least, overwhelming public praise for the black British actor, David Oyelowo, for portraying Dr. Martin Luther King Jr. in the film, *Selma*. In another revealing investigation in 2012, the *Los Angeles Times* reported that in the Academy's membership, "of the nearly 6,000 members, 94 percent are white, 77 percent are male and 86 percent are age 50 or older."[7]

One can easily imagine the ramifications from having whiteness or white maleness as the dominant symbol for American culture and especially for its youths who do not "fit" such an image. One can feel like a misfit, abnormal, or incapable of achieving importance or, even worse, attaining worth in this society. On rare occasions, some individuals are able to break through the invisible ceiling without completely giving in to such socializations. More often than not, however, many young people figure out the formula and begin to emulate this whiteness in order to be accepted. The American media perpetuate the problem for women, for instance, by setting a normative standard of beauty that reduces the concept of attractiveness to a nearly unattainable bodily stereotype of "Anglo-European whiteness, thinness, buxomness, and curviness." Because these qualities are unrealistic and unreachable, the mainstream media and advertisements regularly use preproduction techniques (extreme makeovers, surgeries) and postproduction techniques (airbrushing and computer-generated modifications) to make alterations.[8] Such a culture of "beauty perfectionism" and objectification has been "linked to findings that show young

---

7. Horn et al., "Unmasking the Academy"; Siegel, "Oscar."

8. Frechette, "Beauty and Body Image," 16–17. Cf. Tran, "Cosmetic Surgery," 245–66.

girls' self-esteem plummeting after they are exposed to airbrushed images."[9]

I certainly experienced something similar as a young man when I responded to the question, "Why don't you have more Korean friends?" with "Because I can do better!" The intention of that answer was not to say that Asians or Koreans were inferior but that I was confident in breaking through to the mainstream of society. Nevertheless, the answer is indicative of my acquiescence to the heteronormative white maleness at that time. I wanted to fit in. I wanted to act, dress, and talk like my Caucasian friends.[10] In fact, when I befriended many Caucasian friends and did activities with them, I became more socially, academically, and politically acceptable and successful. The culture rewarded my new "bleached" self with awards, prestigious ranks and positions, opportunities, and popularity. It is difficult, therefore, for anyone, but especially for someone at an impressionable age, not to give up one's cultural, gender, and racial identity when society continues to recompense us for doing so. Like many of these young men of color, including some Korean Americans, I was conflicted yet I allowed American socialization to melt away my identity and have me conform to the American heteronormative white melting pot. I did not imagine alternatives because I was bombarded by images of whiteness or white-maleness. The images that I *did* have available for people of color were foolish, dangerous, objectified, or irresponsible, none of which was the image that I wanted for myself.

Alternative Gender Images

It is unfair to say, however, that all aspects of popular American culture "box in" all individuals in America. While the dominant language, image, and practices of American culture are largely

---

9. Frechette, "Beauty and Body Image," 19. Says Mackey-Kallis: "Objectification theory asserts that media, by articulating the centrality of women's bodies and appearance to identity, socialize self-objectification while contributing to feelings of anxiety and shame" ("Gender Embodiment," 142).

10. See Chiang, "I Tried It."

white and male, recent developments suggest that we are no longer on a singular trajectory. Magazines, commercials, and TV shows have begun to make concerted efforts to use alternative gender images.

Markedly different from the dominant trends in the male-centered gender message, some magazines are taking charge either by addressing objectification and modification of women or by having specific policies to reduce or prohibit artificial modification of images of their models. The bi-monthly Verily, for example, launched in June 2013, is the first "no-Photoshop" fashion magazine. The two female founders vowed to never alter the body or face of its models, in order to celebrate the best of who that model is.[11] More popularly, and perhaps more importantly since its targeted audience is much younger, the editor-in-chief of Seventeen magazine wrote a "Body Peace Treaty" that vowed not to digitally alter the body size or face shapes of young women.[12] Also, model Jennifer Hawkins, Miss Universe 2004, used her fame to raise awareness and joined the anti-Photoshopping movement by posing nude and un-airbrushed on the cover of Marie Claire magazine.[13]

There are some positive signs in TV advertisements as well. Most notable is the "Like a Girl" campaign by Always feminine products. It debunks the connotation that has traditionally accompanied the phrase (i.e. throw like a girl, hit like a girl, etc.) and subverts it by redefining it into positive affirmations. Thus, the commercial displays young female athletes who can throw/run/hit like a girl and be successful and it encourages them to lead like a girl. There are other similar examples in contemporary commercials that promote strong girls and women. The "Girls Can" by

11. "Verily Magazine's No-Photoshop Policy," Huffington Post, Huffpost Style, October 10, 2013, http://www.huffingtonpost.com/2013/10/10/verily-magazine-no-photoshop_n_4079217.html.

12. Haughney, "Seventeen Magazine," The New York Times, July 3, 2012, http://mediadecoder.blogs.nytimes.com/2012/07/03/after-petition-drive-seventeen-magazine-commits-to-show-girls-as-they-really-are/?_r=0.

13. "Nude Model Goes Un-airbrushed" Huffington Post, Huffpost Style, March 18, 2010, http://www.huffingtonpost.com/2010/01/04/nude-model-goes-un-airbru_n_410609.html.

CoverGirl cosmetics, which talks about things girls have been told they cannot do but do anyway, and the campaign to stop saying sorry by Pantene hair products, which asks girls not to apologize where it does not apply, are a couple of non-heteronormative-white-male examples that send messages to girls and women to be strong and successful.[14] Some recent studies even suggest that the visibility of strong women on TV has some positive effects, including its reduction of sexually violent media.[15]

Some modern dads on TV edge outside of the "Men Box" and display characteristics that are less limiting and more creative, attentive, and nurturing. ABC's *Modern Family* exemplifies the range of fatherhood that men are capable of handling. NBC's *Parenthood* features Joel, a nurturing father who is a stay-at-home dad, and Julia, a lawyer and the breadwinner of the family. Such extended meanings of fatherhood allow the imagination to ask whether that range can be expanded to include Asian American families as part of the normative form of the American family. Presented with this televised form of the family, an Asian American man can recognize that he need not feel inadequate about what was previously perceived as a deficiency of fatherhood (bringing in less income than the wife or staying home to be a full-time father). Rather, it allows him to appreciate this alternative form of the family that is conducive to a capable and loving fatherhood.[16]

Perceptions of Korean Americans:
The Asian American Box

Helped partly by these efforts, some Korean Americans (Catholics) are able to break through the gender box and attempt to discover and be true to themselves, only to find that they are trapped in another box: the Asian American Box. The American portrayal of Asians, and therefore Asian Americans, often stems from

14. Harrop, "Strong Women," *Triblive*, August 16, 2014, http://triblive.com/lifestyles/morelifestyles/6507021-74/says-women-strong#axzz3SgKRl2RK.

15. Ferguson, "Positive Female Role-Models," 888–99.

16. Goudreau, "The Changing Roles."

orientalism.[17] It is a perception of Asians as being exotic, different, and perhaps even magical. The media feeds into this perception for Korean Asian women by presenting them as erotic, dangerous, or submissive. Conversely, discrediting can also occur by rendering them as asexual and making IQ their only identifiable marker. In fact, *Honey Hill Bunch Dolls* literally had an Asian doll named "I.Q."[18] Korean men, by contrast, are trapped in a box that depicts them as dangerous Yellow Peril (Kim Jung Un), stoic and nerdy men, goofy ninja warrior and performer (PSY), or quiet (and thus unmanly or effeminate) and even asexual.[19] Once Koreans are categorized and differentiated as being outside of the hegemonic metanarrative, they can effectively be boxed in and blocked from advancing in society. Even if they perform the same tasks and execute them better than the rest like a good "model minority," the perception of their work is that it is "too quiet, passive, nerdy, and small," and thus they "fail to exhibit the form of masculinity valued by the dominant American Society," making their work easily dismissible as inconsequential.[20] This "Bamboo Ceiling" blocks their progress. Many highly skilled, highly educated, top-performing Koreans are denied promotion in their workplaces.[21] On a personal note related to all this is that when I started to go into sexual ethics from the perspective of marginalized people of color, I was often told to be careful. The post-colonial theology or "story theology" to which many Asian theologians subscribe are silently considered not worthy or "rigorous enough" by the mainline theological academia.[22] By categorizing this type of work as different, academic hegemony can effectively attempt to discredit some of what I do. My strategy for survival as an academic since

17. Said, *Orientalism*.

18. "Honey Hill Bunch Dolls 1976–1978," dollreference.com, http://www.dollreference.com/mattel_honey_hill_bunch_dolls.html.

19. Cheung, *Articulate Silences*, 2.

20. Ibid., 18. Cf. Hoon Choi, "Gender and Sexuality," 26–27.

21. Hyun, *Breaking Bamboo Ceiling*; see also Fisher, "Piercing the 'Bamboo Ceiling,'"

22. Tan, "Asian American Liberative Ethics," 138–40.

then has been to have one foot in the normative mainline ethical arena and the other in my own Korean heritage with stories of lived experience of the ostracized, discredited, or suppressed.

However, because of social norms I did not always have enough backbone to pursue what I deemed to be important. During my formative years, I, too, was inculcated, pressured, and persuaded by the dominant discourse of America. I was often vexed by my fellow Koreans and Korean American Catholics more specifically when I found them forming cliques consisting solely of Koreans or, at best, mixtures of students from exclusively Asian descent. I thought I "had the personality" to mingle with the mainline crowd. What I failed to recognize was that I was accepted in great part because I was highly critical and demeaning of Koreans and Asians in general, acted silly, and even made racist comments against my own folk. While I made many white friends this way, those who remained as friends are the ones who alerted me of how wrong my behaviors were at the time. I began to appreciate the brutal honesty of these friends and to understand that I played into the dominant culture's thinking that trapped me in the Asian American Box as the "token Asian." Partly as a result of this awakening, I started to identify belittling comments, condescending looks, and subtle gestures of non-acceptance by my "friends." The Korean cliques, I began to see, were a defense mechanism from these experiences that took a part of our dignity away. I refused to acknowledge this because I was so happy to be accepted by the dominant culture. This recognition allowed me to break out of the box and to start discovering my authentic self.

It is inaccurate to claim, however, that American society's portrayal of Asians and Asian Americans unequivocally puts them in an Asian American Box. For example, unlike how the provocative title of the show suggests, *Fresh Off the Boat* is a sitcom that depicts an Asian family that does not necessarily play into the dominant narrative about Asians. Because it is comedy, the show's characters make fun of each other and the jokes do have an Asian overtone, e.g., their Asian accents. Some may find that problematic. In many ways, however, it is like other sitcoms in the mainstream media except that the performers of the show are Asian. Notwithstanding some problems, therefore, the implication of this show airing on a major network during prime time speaks for itself.

Enduring Korean Influence: The Korean Box

Whether or not they are conscious of their heritage or become embarrassed about their identity, Korean Americans cannot fully separate their American identity from their Korean identity. While I acknowledge that Koreans and Korean Americans do not fully identify with each other, they also cannot be fully separated. Thus, the children of the first generation of Korean immigrants in the US are the direct recipients, and their children indirect recipients, of Korean gender constructions. Aside from the American gender expectations that affect Korean American Catholic identity, therefore, one must also consider the gender expectations that migrated from Korea that affect Korean Americans and Korean American Catholics.

Korean gender thinking stems from their deeply rooted Asian, Neo-Confucian cosmology that sees the universe in harmonious eum-yang (commonly known as Yin-Yang), the balance of darkness and light, and hence of women and men, respectively. Eventually, this cosmology became the impetus for the normative ideology of *namjonyeobi* (man is respected and woman is lowly) and *samjongjido* (three subordinations of women).[23] For men, having exemplary study skills and self-control, along with balance, restraint, and, especially, adherence to moral and ritual norms, associated with the higher classes (*yangban,* or even wealthy *chungin,* "middle people"), was to be *daejangbu* (i.e., a manly person) or a true *gunja* (a lofty gentleman or a sage).[24] For women, Korean womanhood, then, is measured by fulfilling duties as a mother and wife (known as *hyeonmoyangcheo,* or wise mother and good wife). Korean women are judged not directly by their performance as

23. Cho, *Korean Woman,* 70–74.
24. Tikhonov, "Masculinizing the Nation," 1041–46.

such, but by the performance of their husbands and their sons.[25] In fact, by the late Joseon period, a common Korean woman was known through the success of her husband and/or sons.[26] Autonomy was a foreign concept to women, as was justice.

The force of these received traditional norms notwithstanding, the dominant vehicle for instilling gender ideals in contemporary Korea remains the compulsory military service for men. A Korean man is not considered a *jinjja sanai* (real man) unless he has fulfilled his military duties. I have written elsewhere that during military service conscripts are inundated with definitions of what makes a *jinjja sanai*: maintenance of male supremacy, rationalization of often undue power, and sex as amusement or entertainment to relieve stress through words, gestures, and actions that belittle women.[27] Soldiers who do not fit neatly into this machismo are often treated abusively. From my personal experience in the Republic of Korea (ROK) Army, I have witnessed and heard commonly used phrases for what many deemed as "unmanly" men, including "At least a real man should . . ." "Why don't you act like a man?" and "If you are born with something between your legs, act like it!" and the greatest insult of them all, "Are you a girl?"[28] These gender expectations and constructions go beyond the walls of their military posts after men are done with their service. Many men, who may have wielded a terrific amount of power in the military, often unconsciously crave that power. It is no wonder that many men exercise and promote militaristic ethos and strict gender dimorphism in their workplaces, families, and even churches.

In contemporary Korea, these sources of inculcation are manifested in complex and more complicated ways. One of these exhibitions is the way married women are perceived. When

25. Cho, *Korean Woman*, 78–86.

26. In many ways, mothers are still valued by the success of their husbands and sons. Although the obsession in today's Korea over their children's success has sometimes transferred over to fathers and includes their daughters too, these phenomena are very much alive. For example, see Choe, "Mother's Love."

27. Choi, "Brothers in Arms," 79.

28. Ibid.

married women are called *"ajuma,"* people associate that desig-
nation with asexuality. An emblematic representation of this phenomenon is the female custodian in Korea. It is not unusual (and,
in fact, I have experienced this on multiple occasions) for a female
ajuma custodian to walk into a men's restroom in a public building and start cleaning while men are doing their business in the
restroom. In a moment of shock, I looked around to see if anyone
was reacting to this action. I soon noticed that she was not a sexual
being in that society. It was as if she did not exist. It was as if she
were a non-being. Many Korean Americans refer to their mother's
friends as *ajuma*, too and fail to see them as a female being with
full dignity. Rather, they see an *ajuma* as an asexual non-gendered
being. Korean gender norms still operate in the Korean American
Catholic context. When women are expected to do certain chores
around the church strictly based on their gender (be it Sunday
School and Korean school teaching, or nurturing the infants in
the "baby room," or leading youth groups, working in the kitchen,
etc.) the American and Korean gender constructions are active.
Korea may be far removed from where Korean Americans live but
the invisible hand of influence is still very much operative.

Roman Catholic Gender Expectations:
The Catholic Box

The Roman Catholic Church's commitment to human dig-
nity and the life affirming sensibility *can* contribute to enhancing
the American and Korean norms about gender and ethnic justice.
Informed by the Roman Catholic Social Teachings, therefore, Korean American Roman Catholics can "unbox" the women/men/
Asian boxes that have confined them over the years. However, a
part of that process must come from the Church's self-criticism
and reflection. How are Catholics not only enhancing the life and
upholding the dignity of each human being but also perpetuating
the gendered and raced boxes? What polices, practices, or ideas
harm the Korean American gendered selves? I suggest that one
area in which Korean and Korean American Catholic application

of gender injustice is maintained is through gender complementarity. This notion, which was meant to encourage mutual subjugation and sacrifice, is often unbalanced and limiting in practice.

Gender complementarity fundamentally claims that all men and women possess qualities and characteristics specific to their sex, and are *essentially* different from one another. According to the Pontifical Council for the Family, there would be an enormous consequence on a variety of levels if one obscures this exclusive gender binary (John McCarthy's term), including calling into question the traditional norms for the family, "in its natural two-parent structure of mother and father, and make homosexuality and heterosexuality virtually equivalent, in a new model of polymorphous sexuality."[29] If, instead, man and woman actively collaborated (or "complemented") between the sexes, both would enhance each other by filling the gender qualities and characteristics that the other gender is lacking.[30] Likewise, men and women are born with internal and external organs that complement and perfect each other (via procreation).[31] Resulting from the *physical* complementarity, the Pontifical Council for the Family further claims that men and women are hardwired to complement each other in all aspects—including physical, emotional, psychological, spiritual, and relational and social realms.[32] The implication is that a true balance is created between a man and a woman to do what they are naturally equipped to do: to procreate and to properly rear children.[33]

As a model, however, gender complementarity may be too simplistic to explain the complex spectrum of gender and sexuality. Because of the essential and physical nature of this

29. McCarthy, "Binary Gender in Catholic Thought," 2.

30. ". . . the Church, enlightened by faith in Jesus Christ, speaks instead of *active collaboration* between the sexes precisely in the recognition of the difference between man and woman" (ibid., 4).

31. See Salzman and Lawler, *Sexual Person*, 140–45.

32. Ibid., 127–38, and 145–50.

33. Ibid., 138–50. The summary of the types of sexual complementarity is found in the Congregation for the Doctrine of the Faith's (CDF), *Unions between Homosexual Persons*.

complementary model, some aspects of the model contributes to the existing injustice. One of the difficulties that results from this model's biological and ontological destiny is that "women as mothers have an irreplaceable role."[34] While the Catholic Church does allow for women for some public functions,[35] females are essentially more inclined for domestic functions rather than public and leadership positions.[36] Similarly, while the absence of a father in the family is strongly condemned as it "causes psychological and moral imbalance and notable difficulties in family relationships,"[37] the "family-first" boldness that you see in relation to mothers in church documents is hardly present with fathers.[38] When it *is* present, often it is idealized to suggest that a father, as a Christian, should take a job that promotes the unity and stability of the family, as if many men have such luxurious options when choosing a job.[39] Associating men with public work, expecting men to be "manly" breadwinners, often results in their value being measured by their paycheck. Furthermore, making fecundity a requirement for motherhood *vis-à-vis* single(d), infertile, or homosexual persons, is a continual discussion that the Church needs to have with parish priests, experts, and ordinary Catholic folks with their lived experiences.

34. John Paul II, *Laborem exercens*, 19.

35. John Paul II, *Familiaris consortio*, 23: "'There is no doubt that the equal dignity and responsibility of men and women fully justifies women's access to public functions.'"

36. "It implies first of all that women be significantly and actively present in the family, 'the primordial and, in a certain sense sovereign society'" (Pontifical Council for the Family, *On the Collaboration of Man and Woman*, 13).

37. John Paul II, *Familiaris consortio*, 25.

38. For example, the emphasis on "women who freely desire will be able to devote the totality of their time to the work of the household without being stigmatized by society or penalized financially, while those who wish also to engage in other work may be able to do so with an appropriate work-schedule, and not have to choose between relinquishing their family life or enduring continual stress, with negative consequences for one's own equilibrium and the harmony of the family" hardly highlighted men (Pontifical Council for the Family, *On the Collaboration of Man and Woman*, 13).

39. John Paul II, *Familiaris consortio*, 25.

Korean Catholic priests, all of whom have fulfilled compulsory military service in Korea—keeping in mind that the majority of priests who serve Korean American Catholic communities are from Korea—are reaffirmed by exclusive gender binarity to persist in their "soft authoritarian" and hegemonic fashion and sometimes to demand complete loyalty from their parishioners.[40] Notwithstanding a "few good men," these gender norms perpetuate an attitude of male superiority. The time has come to reexamine this model, at the very least, so that a supplementary model is developed that takes unitive function (love) between the sexes more seriously. While the Second Vatican Council (*Gaudium et spes*, for example) intended and clearly denoted unitive function on an equal footing with the procreative function exclusively in the context of marriage, there is no reason why this teaching cannot be extended to a general context of the relationship between men and women and among them.[41] If we do so, it may be possible to encourage a model that not only helps men and women to complement each other based on their gender traits but also on the basis of their taste, preference, and talent. An expansive model would not only be in touch with reality but also be psychologically healthier for all members of the church community.

Emerging From Confusion
as Korean American Catholics

Rather than be inhibited and impeded by the constraints from external forces, Korean American Catholics can be empowered by their multifaceted identities, the very identities that cradle their anxiety. In other words, the very socio-religious and cultural norms that oppress and suppress Korean American Catholics to become "non-beings" in our society, can be the vehicle through which they become a new being.[42] But how? How can Korean

40. Choi, "Brothers in Arms," 82.

41. Paul VI, *Gaudium et spes*, 29, 48–49, 60.

42. Elizondo, *Future Is Mestizo*, 18. See also Kim, *Immigration of Theology*, 50–51.

American Catholics transcend through the very socio-religious and cultural backgrounds that often restrict them? What theological concepts allow Korean American Catholics to imagine a life beyond these borders? I suggest that we can all be empowered not only by the doctrine of *imago dei*—that we are created in the image and likeness of God—but also by the doctrine of Trinity, that God is in relationships, who is multifaceted in one harmonious essence and who created us in that image, in other words, *imago trinitatis*.[43] That is, Korean American Catholics have the distinctive opportunity to embrace their multilayered and authentic selves, to realize that those aspects of the self are gifts from and of God, and to welcome and encourage others to embrace the multiple dimensions of their equally authentic identities. Beyond the distractions and social constructions, then, Korean American Catholics must discover the "spark" from the triune God that *dances* in the depth of our being and notice, embrace, and celebrate it as a free gift (grace) from God.[44] For Korean American Catholics, then, the task is to imitate what this trinity does and learn to dance harmoniously among the different layers of their identities so that they notice, embrace, and celebrate who they are authentically and integrally.

For Korean American Catholic girls and women, therefore, it means that they must struggle to pierce through the women box with the ethnic, cultural, and religious weight on top of it and do so by discovering their God-given grace and dignity. Advocating and

43. Clark, *Vision of Catholic Social Thought*, 105. Clark uses this term in the context of Catholic social teaching and social justice by "examining human dignity through the lens of the Trinity that makes relationality an integral component of the *imago dei*." I extend the concept not only to an external relationality of our human society but also an internal relationality of individuals with the multifaceted nature of our being.

44. The Cappadocian Fathers (such as Basil the Great, Gregory of Nyssa, and Gregory of Nazianzus) employed the term *perichoresis* to describe the relationship among the three persons of the Trinity "as that of an 'ecstatic dance' in which God the Father, Son, and Holy Spirit 'stand outside themselves' and yet 'evoke the life of their divine counterparts'" (Kamitsuka, *Embrace of Eros*, 343). See also Marshall, "Participating in the Life of God," 145. Greek theologian John Damascene in the eighth century also uses *perichoresis* to emphasize the dynamic character of each person in the Trinity; see LaCugna, *God for Us*, 270.

fully embracing one's *imago dei* can counter the part of our socio-religious culture that denigrate women as solely domestic, sexual objects, and dangerous, and doubly so for Korean Asian women as they are seen as submissive, exotic/erotic, and cunning. However, one should not do so by dismissing or disowning their ethnic, cultural, and religious heritage. While their heritage is not perfect, as no sinful human reality is, Korean American Catholic women can arise out of sin and be "resurrected" into a new being in the very context from which their sins came: the Korean American Catholic context. Embracing the goodness and gifts of their tradition, Korean American Catholic women can dance again, emulating the Trinitarian dance among the three persons of Trinity, by noticing, embracing, celebrating their Korean, American, and Catholic gifts. That is a way to fully accept God's grace and the God that made all women in the Trinitarian God's image: *imago trinitatis*.

Imagine, for example, our socio-religious and cultural institutions upholding and celebrating the full value and dignity of women. Such a celebration would bring a world of difference to a young Korean American Catholic girl who excels in school. Rather than seeing her as a threat, a nerd, a "model minority," or unwomanly, her gifts would be praised, admired, and encouraged. Imagine a female Korean American Catholic youth from a poor family with a beautiful single eyelid and darker complexion who aspires to be an accountant, a soccer player, or an engineer. Imagine when, instead of our institutions seeing her as asexual and dangerous or telling her she must be more exotic, sexy, and submissive to succeed, sometimes even to the point of telling her to get plastic surgery or not to pursue her dreams, she is told that she, her talents, and her family are all gifts of and from God to flourish in, and to be shared with, God's human and non-human communities. Imagine a middle-age Korean American Catholic woman who has bicultural, bilingual, organizational, and sharp observation skills. Imagine if, instead of telling her that there is no place for an *ajuma* in the church parish council and at most she can serve as the head of a "mothers group" in charge of the kitchen, or CCD/education related positions, she is told that she is a being with full dignity and her insights and skills are exactly what is needed in the leadership positions in the church to address and contest the falling number in church membership within Korean American Catholic churches and the wider church. Imagine telling a Korean American Catholic wife, whose husband is admired in their Korean American Catholic community for going beyond his masculine borders by working fulltime and still managing to do the dishes and laundry, some cooking and cleaning while also taking care of their children, that we have failed to acknowledge the fact she has *already* been doing *all* of that for years without proper recognition and gratitude because it is "naturally expected" for a "proper" mother to sacrifice. Imagine an elderly Korean American Catholic female member in the church who has seen the world change during her lifetime; if instead of simply giving her rides and lip service and occasionally asking for help in the kitchen, the church gave her a voice so that the community could listen and learn from her wisdom resulting from her experience. Imagine telling her that she is the living memory of the Korean American Catholic Church. Imagine all the possibilities for Korean American Catholics' growth, not only in the size of the membership but also personally, communally, and spiritually. All this is made impossible often because of assumptions about Korean American Catholic women's gender expectations that limit Korean American Catholic women's full flourishing, resulting from the socio-religious and cultural role assignments according to their sex.

For Korean American Catholic boys and men, therefore, it means that they, too, must struggle to break through the men box with the ethnic, cultural, and religious weight pressing down on it and do so by discovering their God-given grace and dignity. This discovery is impossible if Korean American Catholic men are stuck in their boxes and give in to the socio-culturally and religiously constructed version of men by solely being aggressive, childish, stoic, and dominant. If we sit back and let American cultural norms dominate those in the margins, Korean American Catholics will always be seen as dangerous, nerdy, goofy, unmanly, and asexual. However, trying to break free from these constraints through "hypermasculine" reactions or becoming Caucasian only solidifies the "Bamboo Ceiling," and Korean American Catholics who so do will never be considered a "real men" or real "Americans."[45] Again, while Korean, American, and Catholic cultures *can* be constraints, the problems from these forces pale in comparison to the goodness found in these traditions. So how then can Korean American Catholic men dance (and yes, it is not only okay but actually healthy for men to dance!) the Trinitarian dance and notice, embrace, and celebrate their Korean, American, and Catholic gifts?

The first task is to recognize that they are trapped in these invisible boxes. That means that Korean American Catholic men must realize that Korean American Catholic boys "became" boys every time their parents dressed them in blue, excessively differentiated them from girls, gave them military or sports toys, or told them that "boys don't cry."[46] Korean American Catholic men must also recognize that they are not asexual or unmanly because some of them do not wear baggy clothes or because they are interested in wearing colorful clothes or like to listen to K-pop (Korean Pop) music or watch Korean dramas. Moreover, the pressure to become more aggressive and score a leadership position within the Church council is simultaneously a result, in part, of gender socialization and a contributing factor in perpetuating unjust and unhealthy notions of masculinity. In terms of the Korean American Catholic churches, then, rather than saying that Catholic Christian liturgies, confessions, or spirituality are too "feminine" and hence they must be masculinized to grow the church's male membership by holding more golf tournaments and involve more alcohol in the church's regional gatherings (*Gooyeok Moim*), for example, Korean American Catholic men must promote healthier and, indeed, more Christian approaches to the inner and outer growth of their communities.

45. Lee, "Hmong American Masculinities."

46. Chu's observation of a Korean American boy, Min-Haeng, connects to this socialization in many interesting ways. See Chu, *When Boys Become Boys.*

Imagine, for example, our socio-religious and cultural institutions telling Korean American Catholic men that they do not have to "become" someone else to be accepted and loved, rather that they are already lovable and are a gift to this society and of God. Such an acknowledgment and encouragement would make a world of difference to a young Korean American Catholic boy with a beautiful single eyelid and shorter/skinnier stature who excels in nonaggressive activities or shows talent in humanities or in the arts. Rather than seeing him as unmanly or asexual, or weak, his gifts would be praised, admired, and encouraged. Just imagine a male Korean American Catholic youth who listens to hip-hop music, plays classical instruments, or enjoys reading, when, instead of our institutions telling him that he has to listen to "mainstream" music, watch and play football, or become more aggressive to fit in, he is told that he is already lovable and a gift of and from God. Imagine a college-aged Korean American Catholic man who, instead of being told that he has to be childish, make fun of his own ethnicity, and "conquer" non-Asian girls, he is told that he does not have to compromise who he is, or where he came from, to be genuinely "masculine," and that his talents and his honest perspective from socio-religious, racial, cultural oppression is exactly what is needed to make our planet a better place in which all human and non-human beings can flourish. Imagine a recent male Korean American Catholic graduate facing an uncertain job market, who, rather than being told he must not show emotions or any signs of fear, or admit his anxiety, he is told that everyone in his shoes is scared about future uncertainties, fears failure, and can benefit from acknowledging and talking about such anxieties with his loved ones. Imagine telling him that spirituality and needing religious healing is not a sign of weakness but an acknowledgment of human sinfulness, frailty, and restlessness that often leads to a sounder awareness of one's authentic self and to a more peaceful heart. Imagine telling a middle-aged Korean American Catholic man that he did not fail because he did not become a CEO or get a promotion, or was not elected as president of his church's parish council, but rather that his success is measured by how loving, caring, and responsible he is to his family, his surrounding environment, and, indeed, the least of God's people. Imagine telling a Korean American Catholic priest that he is not admired for his manliness that is characterized by non-compromising hierarchal (Neo-Confucian) attitudes, sometimes childish and militaristic authoritativeness, but for his ability to contextualize his ministry, nurturing a community atmosphere of open dialogue, and ushering in a loving ethos even at the risk of being seen as "unmanly" by society at large. Imagine telling an elderly Korean American Catholic man that he is not a "toothless/clawless tiger" (a Korean saying), but an important contributing member and the living memory of his Korean American Catholic community.

Imagine if we enabled Korean American Catholic women and men to roam and dance freely through their God-given, multilayered identities; it would help them transcend many obstacles that confine them to their boxes. If we cannot imagine it, we will remain in our boxes, telling ourselves that this box is not so bad, that this situation is fair, and, ultimately convince ourselves that there are no boxes. If we cannot imagine it, our chances to notice, embrace, and celebrate our multilayered dignified self will never become a reality. However, if we are just stuck imagining, it simply becomes a fantasy. A full embracing of human dignity must be carried out on the most basic and practical level in all Korean American Catholic communities and beyond. If God is a dancing Trinity in celebration, God must also want us to dance *with* God. For Korean American Catholics to do so, the leaders of religious institutions and families must help young Korean American Catholic women and men to overcome some obstacles—i.e. their labeling of emotions, conversation, and cooperation as not masculine; or of rational, active, and authoritative qualities as not feminine or Asian. Simultaneously, however, we must encourage them to lead from what we have labeled as strictly masculine or feminine values: rationality, intelligence, ambition, *and* poignancy, empathy, and care. All these characteristics can be, regardless of color, gender, or religion, vehicles through which the grace of God can be made more visible in our lives. Restricting them would not only be individually and institutionally detrimental, but would also limit their God-given human capacity to live more authentically, most honestly, and more fully. After all, St. Irenaeus taught us, *Gloria dei est vivens homo*. The Glory of God is when human beings are (fully) alive.

Conclusion

The struggle remains: this project is a telling example of Korean American gender reality and, more particularly, Korean American Catholic gender reality. It was difficult to find, for example, female contributors and when we did find some people, there was no interest, or at least no expressed interest, in joining the project at hand. Unfortunately, one such contributing member who was part of this project had to discontinue for personal reasons. Thus, this chapter serves not only as a critique of society and culture but also, perhaps more importantly for us, as a tool and a reminder of the need for introspection. What can Korean American Catholics do to bring about conditions that allow them to live more fully as Korean American Catholics? This task still remains.

One way to initiate our steps toward the right, Catholic, direction is to pay attention to God's creation and see if God is already telling us what to do in and through it. More specifically to this chapter, then, we can start by paying attention to what our bodily, psychologically, and emotionally gendered selves are telling us. There are elements of the unexpected and surprise in our bodies that humble us to the point of acknowledging that we are not in control. That fact remains that as we become adolescents, adults, middle-aged, and elderly, our bodies change. In the process of that change, we become worried, anxious, and vulnerable. However, Korean American Catholics can find their comfort in knowing that in every stage of life there is meaning and reason to celebrate these changes as a part of a growing process, bodily, socially, and spiritually. These different experiences and aspects of one's gendered self, including but not limited to puberty, growing pains, menstruation (menarche), sperm producing (semenarche), development of breasts, bodily hair, change of voice, pregnancy, gestation, being in labor, birthing, wrinkling, hair loss, graying, menopause, erectile dysfunction, increase or decrease of estrogen or androgen, reduction of sight and sound, the slowdown of the digestive and immune system, etc., are layers of one's being that enable us to grow in wisdom, humility, and ultimately a better understanding of God's gift and will.

One's gender reality, then, is multifaceted and complicated. We do not always understand or control our gendered being. However, Christian Catholics live from a conviction that all this, even with suffering and inconsistencies, is made in the image and likeness of God. A diverse aspect of our sexual body and gendered self is all a gift from God. We are, and our bodies are, sacred. All the ways in which our bodies are active, assertive, leading, and powerful *and* in which our bodies are receiving, nurturing, guiding, and soft are sacred. While there are heteropatriarchal powers that distort our vision of reality, we must dance the Trinitarian dance and notice, embrace, and celebrate these wonderful, sometimes painful, aspects of who we are. For Korean American Catholics, whose gendered identities come in cultured and raced baggage, they, too, must realize that, instead of the heteropatriarchal society that tells them there is only one way of being accepted, that they are to dance among their Korean, American, and Catholic realms and celebrate the multiple aspects of their gendered raced identities and lead from their true selves. This authentic life of young Korean American Catholics can be the primary example that serves as a corrective to the non-Christian world and to our own Catholic world in leading the path to living an authentic, integral, and truer self.

If we paid attention to Jesus, the Nazarene who crossed his borders with his multiple identities, we would already know all this. Jesus did not just take charge with his 12 disciples but with a number of named and unnamed women. Jesus took care of people who were considered outcasts. He denounced elitism and irresponsible exercise of social power. He nurtured and wept for the oppressed. He was unmanly by his societal norms, and he helped people who were considered unmanly, therefore, unworthy. Indeed he would be considered abnormal by our norms today. He would be an ostracized Korean American Catholic, like many of us today. However, he led from the harmonious dance of his diverse self. He did not stop celebrating. He was empowered by his multiplicity and he owned it. As a result, the person of Jesus himself became, not confusion among many identities, but a unifying grace for others to see and learn.

Is this not the task of all Korean American Catholics? As shown in the section, "alternative gender images" earlier, Korean American Catholic churches must also make visible the fullness of who we are, especially in young Korean American Catholics. The socio-religious and cultural institutions, which often distort what *is* and confuse many of us, can become foundations for grace. When we are empowered by Korean, American, and Catholic traditions and own them through our struggles and dances, it would unify all of us by revealing the image of God in us. By noticing, embracing, and celebrating our true selves, we can live a life of joy, responsibility, and selfless love that is inclined toward the service of others, especially the ones most in need. In this way, Korean American Catholics can become an important contributing part of a wider Christian body and, certainly, a participating member of the Mystical Body. Jesus' stories have been preaching this message to his disciples, and therefore to all of us, all along. Our bodies and our very being have been telling us this all along. We are simply not aware because we are often blinded by limiting social, familial, and, indeed, religious constructions. When God's creation is living to their fullest selves, when we truly humanize each other to our fullest potential, we will truly make God visible, present, and alive in our lives. What Korean American Catholics, and all of us, need to do (to borrow Pope Francis' message to Koreans during his monumental visit in 2014) is to "Wake up!" When we are awake, when we realize God's message being told through us, when we finally love ourselves, we will truly rejoice in hope. When we are awake and when the relationship among our multiple identities are in harmonious flow, we will begin to see that *imago trinitatis* extends to harmonious relationships among all Korean American Catholic communities and, indeed, all of human communities as One Body with many parts.[47] Let us notice the goodness, then, in all of our selves. Let us love our Korean, American, and Catholic selves. Let us learn from our Triune God and rejoice, and dance!

47. "Understanding the *imago dei* as *imago trinitatis* requires that each individual human person is in the image and likeness of God, and that *we*, as a community, are in the image and likeness of God." Clark, *Vision of Catholic Social Thought*, 105.

Bibliography

Cheung, King-Kok. *Articulate Silences: Hisaye Yamamoto, Maxine Hong Kingston, Joy Kogawa.* Ithaca, NY: Cornell University Press, 1993.

Chiang, Sharline. "I Tried It . . . Being White." *OZY*, May 25, 2015. http://www.ozy.com/true-story/i-tried-it-being-white/38961.

Cho, Hye Jung. *Hankookui yeoseonggwa namseong* [Korean Woman and Man]. Seoul: Munhakgwa Jiseongsa, 1988.

Choe, Sang-Hun. "Mother's Love Becomes Obsession for Some South Koreans." *New York Times*, Asia Pacific Section, June 10, 2009. http://www.nytimes.com/2009/06/10/world/asia/10iht-skater.html?scp=3&sq=Korean%20mothers&st=cse.

Choi, Hoon. "Brothers in Arms and Brothers in Christ?: The Military and the Catholic Church as Sources for Modern Korean Masculinity." *Journal of the Society of Christian Ethics* 32, no. 2 (2012) 75–92.

———. "Gender and Sexuality." In *Asian American Christian Ethics: Voices, Methods, Issues*, edited by Grace Y. Kao and Ilsup Ahn, 19–39. Waco, TX: Baylor University Press, 2015.

Chu, Judy Y. *When Boys Become Boys: Development, Relationships, and Masculinity.* New York: New York University, 2014.

Clark, Meghan J. *The Vision of Catholic Social Thought: Virtue of Solidarity and the Praxis of Human Rights.* Minneapolis: Fortress, 2014.

Congregation for the Doctrine of the Faith. *Considerations Regarding Proposals to Give Legal Recognition to Unions between Homosexual Persons.* June 3, 2003. http://www.vatican.va/roman_curia/congregations/cfaith/documents/rc_con_cfaith_doc_20030731_homosexual-unions_en.html.

Elizondo, Virgilio. *Future Is Mestizo: Life where Cultures Meet.* Boulder, CO: University Press of Colorado, 2000.

Frechette, Julie. "Beauty and Body Image: Beauty Myths." In *Encyclopedia of Gender in Media*, edited by Mary Kosut, 16–20. Washington, DC: Sage, 2012.

———. "Gender and Femininity: Motherhood." In *Encyclopedia of Gender in Media*, edited by Mary Kosut. Washington, DC: Sage, 2012.

Ferguson, Christopher J. "Positive Female Role-Models Eliminate Negative Effects of Sexually Violent Media." *Journal of Communication* 62, no. 5 (October 2012) 888–99.

Goudreau, Jenna. "The Changing Roles of TV Dads." *Forbes*, June 15, 2010. http://www.forbes.com/2010/06/15/tv-dads-parenthood-modern-family-forbes-woman-time-dean-mcdermott.html.

Harrop, JoAnne Klimovich. "Strong Women, Strong Ads: Marketers Target Female Empowerment." *Triblive*, August 16, 2014. http://triblive.com/lifestyles/morelifestyles/6507021-74/says-women-strong#axzz3SgKRl2RK.

Haughney, Christine. "Seventeen Magazine Vows to Show Girls 'as They Really Are.'" *New York Times*, Media Decoder (blog), July 3, 2012. http://

mediadecoder.blogs.nytimes.com/2012/07/03/after-petition-drive-seventeen-magazine-commits-to-show-girls-as-they-really-are/?_r=0.

Horn, John, et al. "Unmasking the Academy: Oscar Voters Overwhelmingly White, Male." *Los Angeles Times,* February 19, 2012. http://www.latimes.com/entertainment/envelope/oscars/la-et-unmasking-oscar-academy-project-20120219-story.html#page=1.

Huffington Post Staff. "Nude Model Goes Un-airbrushed on Marie Claire Cover," *Huffington Post,* Huffpost Style, last updated May 25, 2011. http://www.huffingtonpost.com/2010/01/04/nude-model-goes-un-airbru_n_410609.html.

———. "Verily Magazine's No-Photoshop Policy Proves It Can Be Done." *Huffington Post,* Huffpost Style, October 14, 2013. http://www.huffingtonpost.com/2013/10/10/verily-magazine-no-photoshop_n_4079217.html.

Hyun, Jane. *Breaking Bamboo Ceiling: Career Strategies for Asians.* New York: HarperCollins, 2006.

John Paul II (pope). *Familiaris consortio.* November 22, 1981. http://w2.vatican.va/content/john-paul-ii/en/apost_exhortations/documents/hf_jp-ii_exh_19811122_familiaris-consortio.html.

———. *Laborem exercens.* September 14, 1981. http://w2.vatican.va/content/john-paul-ii/en/encyclicals/documents/hf_jp-ii_enc_14091981_laborem-exercens.html.

Kamitsuka, Margaret D., ed. *The Embrace of Eros: Bodies, Desires, and Sexuality in Christianity.* Minneapolis: Fortress, 2010.

Kim, Simon C. *An Immigration of Theology: Theology of Context as the Theological Method of Virgilio Elizondo and Gustavo Gutiérrez.* Eugene, OR: Wipf and Stock, 2012.

LaCugna, Catherine Mowry. *God for Us: The Trinity and Christian Life.* San Francisco: HarperCollins, 1991.

Lee, Stacey J. "Hmong American Masculinities." In *Adolescent Boys: Exploring Diverse Cultural of Boyhood,* edited by Niobe Way and Judy Y. Chu, 13–31. New York: New York University Press, 2004.

Mackey-Kallis, Susan. "Gender Embodiment." In *Encyclopedia of Gender in Media,* edited by Mary Kosut, 141–46. Washington, DC: Sage, 2012.

Marshall, Molly. "Participating in the Life of God: A Trinitarian Pneumatology." *Perspectives in Religious Studies* 30, no. 2 (2003) 139–50.

McCarthy, John. "Binary Gender in Catholic Thought." In *God, Science, Sex, Gender: An Interdisciplinary Approach to Christian Ethic,* edited by Patricia Beattie Jung and Aana Marie Vigen, 123–39. Urbana: University of Illinois Press, 2010.

Paul VI (pope). *Gaudium et spes.* December 7, 1965. http://www.vatican.va/archive/hist_councils/ii_vatican_council/documents/vat-ii_const_19651207_gaudium-et-spes_en.html.

Pontifical Council for the Family. *On the Collaboration of Man and Woman.* (2004). http://www.vatican.va/roman_curia/congregations/cfaith/documents/rc_con_cfaith_doc_20040731_collaboration_en.html.

Said, Edward. *Orientalism.* New York: Pantheon, 1978.

Salzman, Todd A., and Michael G. Lawler. *The Sexual Person: Toward a Renewed Catholic Anthropology.* Washington, DC: Georgetown University Press, 2008.

Siegel, Tatiana. "Oscars: Acting Nominees All White." *The Hollywood Reporter,* January 15, 2015. http://www.hollywoodreporter.com/news/oscars-acting-nominees-all-white-764018.

Tan, Sharon M. "Asian American Liberative Ethics." In *Ethics: A Liberative Approach,* edited by Miguel A. De La Torre, 127–42. Minneapolis: Fortress, 2013.

Tarrant, Shira. "Gender and Masculinity: White Masculinity." In *Encyclopedia of Gender in Media,* edited by Mary Kosut, 138–41. Washington, DC: Sage, 2012.

Tikhonov, Vladimir. "Masculinizing the Nation: Gender Ideologies in Traditional Korea and in the 1890s–1900s Korean Enlightenment Discourse." *The Journal of Asian Studies* 66, no. 4 (2007) 1029–65.

Tran, Jonathan. "Cosmetic Surgery." In *Asian American Christian Ethics: Voices, Issues, Methods,* edited by Grace Kao and Ilsup Ahn, 245–68. Waco, TX: Baylor University Press, 2015.

Westerfelhaus, Robert. "Gender and Masculinity: Fatherhood." In *Encyclopedia of Gender in Media,* edited by Mary Kosut, 134–36. Washington, DC: Sage, 2012.

About the Contributors

Introduction
Francis Daeshin Kim

Francis Daeshin Kim is Youth Ministry Coordinator at St. Joseph Korean Catholic Center in the Archdiocese of Los Angeles, and serves as the Vice President of the FIAT Foundation, a national organization whose mission is to empower the Korean American Catholic community. He was born in Seoul, grew up in London and Paris, received degrees in English Literature from the University of Oxford, and currently lives with his wife and two children in Santa Clarita. You can read more about his life and ministry on his blog at http://frankatjoes.com/.

The Emergence of Korean American Catholics: Tracing the Narratives of God's People
Simon C. Kim

Simon C. Kim is Assistant Professor in Theology and the recipient of the Thomas E. Chambers Endowed Professorship in Theology at University of Holy Cross (New Orleans, LA). He is a priest of the Diocese of Orange in Southern California ordained in 1998. Kim completed his doctoral studies at The Catholic University of America (Washington, DC) in Systematic Theology in 2011. In 2013, Kim began formulating both the gathering of Korean American Catholic theologians and this project in anticipation of the jubilee celebration.

Kim was born in Seoul, South Korea and came to the United States at an early age. His own experience of church and identity is the impetus for his theological reflections as he strives to make faith generationally and culturally relevant. His publications, *A World Church in our Backyard: How the Spirit Moved Church and Society, Memory and Honor: Cultural and Generational Ministry to Korean American Communities,* and *An Immigration of Theology: Theology of Context as the Theological Method of Virgilio Elizondo and Gustavo Gutiérrez,* bridge his theological endeavors and pastoral engagements.

The Korean American Catholic Experience as Part of an Ongoing Pentecost

Paul D. Lee

Paul D. Lee is pastor at the Shrine of St. Jude in Rockville, MD. He was the first Korean American diocesan priest ordained in 1983 for the Archdiocese of Washington, DC. Previously, Lee served as the Archdiocesan Director of the Office for Ecumenical & Interreligious Affairs and the Office for Continuing Education for Priests. Lee received an STL and STD from The Pontifical University of Saint Thomas Aquinas (*Angelicum*), Rome, in 1994. His publications include *Bridging: Korean and Korean Americans, Among Christians and Among Religions.*

Immigrating to the United States in 1983 in his twenties allowed Lee to bridge both the Korean and American communities as evident by his posts as the president of the National Korean Pastoral Center for Korean Catholics in the United States and Canada as well as the Korean National Delegate for the USCCB (1999–2004). Lee is also an international speaker on subjects ranging from ecumenism, interreligious dialogue, ecclesiology, and Trinitarian theology. He has been invited to address seminaries, synagogues, mosques, dioceses, ecumenical conferences, and other Christian churches.

Korean American Catholics in the Changing American Religious Landscape: A Statistical Portrait

Chaeyoon Lim

Chaeyoon Lim is Associate Professor of Sociology at the University of Wisconsin-Madison. He attended Seoul National University in South Korea before immigrating to the United States and completing his doctoral studies at Harvard University. Lim specializes in sociology in the public arena ranging from civic engagement, social movements and networks, and religious change. He has authored and co-authored nearly a dozen articles on such topics.

Lim has been the recipient of numerous grants from every institution that he has been associated with to continue the important work of understanding the changing political, social, and religious landscape in the United States as well as in Korea. He has also received high praise and honors for his work including the distinguished article award of the Society for the Scientific Study of Religion in 2011 and the best article award of the American Sociological Association on altruism, morality and social solidarity in 2013.

The Family of God: Resurrection and Eternal Life in Korean Catholicism and the Western Tradition

James K. Lee

James K. Lee serves as Assistant Professor of the History of Early Christianity at the Perkins School of Theology at Southern Methodist University in Dallas, TX. Lee completed his doctoral studies at the University of Notre Dame (IN) in 2012. In addition to his teaching specialties in the history of Christianity, patristic anthropology and soteriology, and monasticism, Lee's research interests include St. Augustine, Latin patristics, ecclesiology, and Biblical exegesis.

Lee has been awarded many professional distinctions including the Kaneb Center Award for Excellence in Teaching at the University of Notre Dame and the Johannes Quasten Scholarship at The Catholic University of America. His publications include "The Church as Mystery in the Theology of Saint Augustine" in *Studia Patristica*, 2013.

Seasons of Belonging: St. Thomas Aquinas as a Guide for Korean American Catholics

Andrew Kim

Andrew Kim is Assistant Professor of Theology at Walsh University (North Canton, OH). He is a third generation bi-racial Korean American and was received into the Catholic Church in 2007. After completing his doctoral studies at The Catholic University of America in 2012, he relocated to the North Canton area with his wife Caitlin, their son Theo, and their four daughters Lucy, Zoë, Phoebe, and Moira. Kim's primary area of study is "Virtue Ethics," which is the component of Catholic moral theology that draws most from the great tradition of Socrates, Plato, Aristotle, Augustine, and Aquinas in order to approach the moral life.

Kim's recent publication, *An Introduction to Catholic Ethics Since Vatican II* provides a comprehensive overview of the development of Catholic ethics in the wake of the Second Vatican Council (1962–1965), an event widely considered crucial to the reconciliation of the Catholic Church and the modern world. Beginning with the moral vision revealed through the person of Jesus Christ and continuing with elaborations on this vision from figures such as Augustine and Aquinas, this volume elucidates the continuity of the Catholic moral tradition.

Imagine! An Examination of Race and Gender in Korean American Catholicism

Hoon Choi

Hoon Choi was born and raised in South Korea and moved to the United States as a youth. He was baptized in the Roman Catholic Church, grew up practicing in the Presbyterian church before deciding to celebrate his confirmation back in the Catholic Church. He fulfilled his compulsory duty as a soldier in the Republic of Korea Army (infantry 2006–2008) in the middle of his doctoral studies. He received his degree from Loyola University (Chicago, IL) in 2012.

His research interests range from (de)constructing norms of masculinities in Christian religions to interdisciplinary dialogue on gendered racial ideologies. These interests resulted in the publication of "Brothers in Arms and Brothers in Christ? The Military and the Catholic Church as Sources for Modern Korean Masculinity" (*Journal of the Society of Christian Ethics*). Choi has presented in scholarly conferences both here in the United States and in South Korea. He is happily married to Theresa Lee who gave birth to their first child, Justin Joonsuh Choi in this jubilee year.